The Mindful Classroom

MINDFULNESS IN EDUCATION

Series Editors: Karen Ragoonaden and Sabre Cherkowski, The University of British Columbia

This interdisciplinary series examines the theoretical and the practical applications of Mindfulness in Education (MIE). Coming from a range of academic disciplines, an increasing number of studies on mindfulness and related contemplative practices underscore the relevance of MIE. Prompted by the robust scientific findings of mindfulness as a tool to support physical, emotional and mental health in adult populations, several initiatives have emerged devoted to applying and evaluating mindfulness in K–12 and in higher education. Teachers are enrolling in mindfulness programs, administrators are introducing mindfulness to their schools, and researchers are devising ways to evaluate the effects of mindfulness in cohorts of students and teachers. In particular, the collected volumes of this series explore the impact of universal practices of mindfulness (being aware, paying attention, noticing, being in the present moment, being non-judgmental) and the attributes that cultivate and support well-being in pedagogical contexts.

The Mindful Classroom: Constructive Conversations on Race, Identity, and Justice
By Tru Leverette
Mindful and Relational Approaches to Social Justice, Equity, and Diversity in Teacher Education
Edited By Julian Kitchen and Karen Ragoonaden
Mindful Alignment: Foundations of Educator Flourishing
By Sabre Cherkowski, Kelly Hanson, and Keith Walker
A Mindful Teaching Community: Possibilities for Teacher Professional Learning
Edited by Kelly Hanson

The Mindful Classroom

Constructive Conversations on Race, Identity, and Justice

Tru Leverette

LEXINGTON BOOKS
Lanham • Boulder • New York • London

Published by Lexington Books
An imprint of The Rowman & Littlefield Publishing Group, Inc.
4501 Forbes Boulevard, Suite 200, Lanham, Maryland 20706
www.rowman.com

86-90 Paul Street, London EC2A 4NE

Copyright © 2022 by The Rowman & Littlefield Publishing Group, Inc.

Tru Leverette, Love and the Illusion of Race: Toward a Politics of Being, *MELUS*, Volume 43, Issue 1, Spring 2018, Pages 183–213, by permission of Oxford University Press.

All rights reserved. No part of this book may be reproduced in any form or by any electronic or mechanical means, including information storage and retrieval systems, without written permission from the publisher, except by a reviewer who may quote passages in a review.

British Library Cataloguing in Publication Information Available

Library of Congress Cataloging-in-Publication Data

ISBN 978-1-7936-3540-2 (cloth)
ISBN 978-1-7936-3542-6 (paper)
ISBN 978-1-7936-3541-9 (electronic)

The Mindful Classroom

Constructive Conversations on Race, Identity, and Justice

Tru Leverette

LEXINGTON BOOKS
Lanham • Boulder • New York • London

Published by Lexington Books
An imprint of The Rowman & Littlefield Publishing Group, Inc.
4501 Forbes Boulevard, Suite 200, Lanham, Maryland 20706
www.rowman.com

86-90 Paul Street, London EC2A 4NE

Copyright © 2022 by The Rowman & Littlefield Publishing Group, Inc.

Tru Leverette, Love and the Illusion of Race: Toward a Politics of Being, *MELUS*, Volume 43, Issue 1, Spring 2018, Pages 183–213, by permission of Oxford University Press.

All rights reserved. No part of this book may be reproduced in any form or by any electronic or mechanical means, including information storage and retrieval systems, without written permission from the publisher, except by a reviewer who may quote passages in a review.

British Library Cataloguing in Publication Information Available

Library of Congress Cataloging-in-Publication Data

ISBN 978-1-7936-3540-2 (cloth)
ISBN 978-1-7936-3542-6 (paper)
ISBN 978-1-7936-3541-9 (electronic)

Contents

Acknowledgments	vii
Preface: Why Be Mindful?	ix
Introduction: Where Have We Been? Where Are We Now? Tracing Civil (and Uncivil) Discourse	xv
1 What We Talk about When We Talk about Race: Encountering Individual Identity, Personal Agency, and Collective Struggle	1
Mindfulness and Movement Practices	15
2 Who and How Will We Be?: Creating Constructive Conversations	23
Mindfulness and Movement Practices	43
3 From Page to Presence: Using Literary Studies to Engage the World	51
Mindfulness and Movement Practices	61
4 Engaging Community	67
Mindfulness and Movement Practices	77
5 The Mindful Classroom: Seeing and Freeing the Whole Student	83
6 Student Voices: Reflections from Mindfully Engaged Students	101
Conclusion: Where Are We Going? Communities to Come	113
Afterword: From Conversation to Commitment *Andrew Woods*	121

Appendix A: How to Be a Trojan Horse: Intervening in Racist
    Conversations   125
Appendix B: The Eight Limbs of Ashtanga Yoga   131
Appendix C: Benefits of *Asana*, *Pranayama*, and Meditation   141
Appendix D: Foundational Yoga Postures   145
Appendix E: Resources   147
Bibliography   149
Index   155
About the Author   159

Acknowledgments

The work of teaching and learning, of identity development, and of justice is never accomplished alone. I am grateful to so many who support my work in these areas.

First, I thank my students for their dedication to learning, their eagerness to engage with others and new ideas, and their courage in sharing themselves. I'm particularly grateful to Michael Coutu, sierra jones-frishman, Deqa Moussa, Kellea Roberson, Matthew Welcome, and Andrew Woods; students like each of these make the classroom truly transformational. I also thank my gifted colleagues at the University of North Florida (UNF). In particular, I would like to thank Writing Group members Felicia Bevel, Nick de Villiers, Chris Gabbard, Stephen Gosden, Laura Heffernan, Jenni Lieberman, Betsy Nies, and Sarah Provost—all of whom have been supportive colleagues offering valuable critiques and encouragement and whose work I admire greatly. Keith Cartwright has also been a great inspiration and support, and I thank him for his affability and skill in fostering a climate of genuine care, respect, and collegiality in our department.

My thanks to the UNF Center for Community-Based Learning for offering the Community Scholars Program. My time in the program was invaluable for helping me understand and appreciate what true community partnership entails and how to foster it. I'm also grateful for those who work in the UNF Center for Research and Instruction Technology; I would be floundering with online teaching without their help and the center's sponsorship of my Master of Online Teaching certification from the University of Illinois. I'm also grateful for and inspired by the work of UNF's Center for Urban Education and Policy, specifically the work of Chris Janson and Rudy Jamison. They, along with my English Department colleague James Beasley, have been outstanding models for engaging students with communities and thereby helping to achieve crucial community goals.

I thank my yoga and meditation teachers who have helped me learn vital lessons about life through these practices. Shri Hamilton-Hubbard and Stan Hubbard of Bliss Yoga Shala guided me early on this path, and I feel blessed to have been their student.

I thank Micky ScottBey Jones, whom I've not had the privilege to meet, for writing the poem "Invitation to Brave Space." I like to share this poem with classes and other discussion groups before we engage in difficult conversations, as it helps us stay mindful of who we are, why we're together, and what our individual and communal work entails. I encourage others to do the same.

I also offer my thanks and love to my mother, Yvonne, who has taught me invaluable lessons about being true and seeking what is right. And countless thanks to Vita—who teaches me daily, sometimes joins me for yoga, and always brings me delight and laughter—and to David—who encourages and stays curious about the work I do, makes me laugh until I cry, and helps me float into the bliss of being in the moment. Thank you both for ushering me out of my head and into life. You both inspire my being and becoming, and I love you infinitely.

And, of course, all thanks to the Divine Indwelling. Yes. Om Shanti.

Preface
Why Be Mindful?

I remember my second-grade classroom very well. Its design was based on the Workshop Way (registered), an educational philosophy founded by Grace H. Pilon that offers a holistic system of learning, recognizing individual learning styles and timelines to achieve academic and life-skill success. Students complete their daily tasks independently, and in our classroom, these tasks were based on a series of activities noted by cards taped along all four classroom walls. There were enough activities that I don't remember ever making it all the way around the room in a single day, but one activity in particular became etched in my memory and a subject of personal contemplation ever since. Each day, every student watched the second hand of our classroom clock for three minutes. Such was the extent of the activity, but what a lesson it became for me. (No doubt, this was how I became such an accurate estimator of what time it is!) For three minutes every day, I was aware of the concept of time—its passage, duration; its fleetingness or length, depending on my mood. I slowed down my "doing" in order to "be," and I practiced one-pointed focus, a meditation practice and avenue toward mindfulness.

There are many types of meditation, and my intention here is not to catalogue each one but to elucidate the usefulness of mindfulness techniques for teachers and students, especially when they are engaging with potentially triggering topics such as race and social justice. In my training as a yoga teacher, I learned in the tradition of transcendental meditation, and this is the meditation I practice daily. I use a mantra, a Sanskrit phrase that was given to me by my teacher and that ends up resonating as just the "blip" of a sound on the edge of my awareness the deeper my meditation goes. In the words of David Frawley, "The word mantra is derived from two Sanskrit words. The first is 'manas' or 'mind' . . . the second [is] 'trai' meaning to 'protect' or to 'free from.' Therefore, the word mantra in its most literal sense means 'to free from the mind.'. . . Mantra is, at its core, a tool used by the mind that eventually frees one from the vagaries of the mind" (Frawley 2010, 6). The unchecked mind shifts and changes like a stormy wind. This is the "monkey mind" discussed in meditation classes, the mind that jumps from one thought-branch to another, following it for a few leaps before jumping onto another branch altogether, without rest. This mind is chaotic and produces chaotic feelings. In contrast, a mind trained to see its own habits can direct itself on where to go. It slows down. It calms. It is aware. The development of these qualities in meditation leads to a mind more capable of focus, of emotional stability rather than reactivity, of conscious choice. And these qualities translate to daily life as mindfulness.

Mindfulness is both a long-standing practice rooted in Hinduism and Buddhism and a contemporary buzz-word. In the United States, the movement's popularization traces to Jon Kabat-Zinn, who in 1979 began the Mindfulness-Based Stress Reduction program at the University of Massachusetts to serve those with chronic illness. Mindfulness can be defined as compassionate awareness of the present moment, but what does that mean? When one is aware of the present moment, they are not living in the past or the future. When one practices compassionate awareness, one is paying attention without judgment to the present moment.

How often have many of us found ourselves reliving the loop of a painful, anger-inducing, or embarrassing moment? When we do, our minds trick us into believing we are in that past moment again—we begin to embody the emotions we feel; we hold our bodies tensely in response to those emotions; we reenact scenarios, even saying the things we wish we'd have said then. This is not present-moment awareness. Alternatively, how many times do we project ourselves into a future that has yet to arrive? We have that job-house-partner-vacation and we drift into the illusion of its reality. This is not present-moment awareness.

Of course, there is a place for positive visualization of what we want the future to look like; after all, we cannot set goals or dream possibilities if we aren't engaging our imaginations. But dreaming, goal setting, and creative visualization aren't always rooted in present-moment awareness, and the difference is our attachment to the outcome. When we live with present-moment awareness, we can imagine endless possibilities, but we simultaneously recognize that the possibilities we imagine might never come to pass: things might remain as they are, or things might become better than we can dream. We can hold positive expectations without being attached to a singular fixed outcome generated through our imagining.

This state of being is part of present-moment awareness. This is where I am. These are the thoughts I am thinking. The emotions I am feeling are based in these thoughts. I am holding my body in specific ways because of these thoughts and feelings. And I can witness whether these thoughts, feelings, and postures are helpful or harmful to me right now—physically, emotionally, and mentally. Based on what I observe, I can choose another thought, feeling, posture. This is present-moment awareness. This is mindfulness.

Many people who begin a meditation and mindfulness practice feel deflated when they can't quiet their monkey minds. But the point of the practice is the *practice*—the repetition of a behavior or activity for the purpose of becoming more proficient at it. The practice of meditation involves a number of steps: first, the growing awareness that the mind is indeed active; second, the nonjudgmental, compassionate awareness that thoughts exist; third, the witnessing of thoughts without emotional reaction; and fourth, the return of awareness to one-pointed focus. We might liken this practice to watching clouds pass. Just like thoughts in our minds, clouds exist in the sky. We can keep our eyes on the sky, noticing the clouds drifting by without letting our eyes follow them. We see the sky, and the clouds pass our field of vision. In the same way, we can watch the screen of our mind (or a candle flame, or the sensations of our breath, or the feeling of our feet on the floor) and notice thoughts passing in and out of our awareness. We don't try to hold the clouds, and we needn't try to hold onto (or follow) the thoughts. This is the practice of meditation. And when we turn this nonjudgmental awareness to our thoughts, feelings, and actions in daily life, we are practicing mindfulness.

One truth of the practice is that the more awareness we develop in meditation, the more aware we become when we're not meditating. The habit and skill of silent witnessing translates into silent witnessing in life, from which we can determine action rather than fall into reaction. As Charles Johnson has written in his collection of essays *Taming the Ox*, "everything in life—each precious moment—is an opportunity for spiritual practice and not to be wasted by a lack of mindfulness, living always in the present moment (for where else is there to live?), not becoming 'stuck' on results, nor to 'hope' or 'despair,' those false polarities that are more about the needs of the fictitious ego, so full of itself, than anything else" (21). Mindfulness practices help us cultivate this ability to be alive in the present moment.

Similarly, yoga practices teach us how to breathe into and exist in what *is* in any given moment. They help us listen to body-based wisdom that can teach us valuable information about our past experiences, including trauma, and our present needs. When used as a therapy, yoga joins the field of bodywork called somatics—those practices that utilize the connection between mind and body to help practitioners observe internal realities signaling pain, discomfort, imbalance, and dis-ease. Such practices can help us observe our conditioned tendencies, including the patterns in which we hold our bodies that may contribute to our dis-ease. This information can show us how we hold past experiences in the body (think about how your shoulders remain tight after a near-accident on the highway), which can then aid in the subsequent release of these experiences and patterns.

Thus, yoga practices help us stretch ourselves—literally and figuratively—as we rest within postures, work through discomfort, and expand our embodied awareness. The physical practices of yoga mimic meditation and become opportunities to contemplate our deeper reality—including our motivations, patterns, and goals—allowing us a profound understanding of ourselves as individuals and in connection with other individuals. Of course, yoga has physiological benefits as well. We know the physical practice can enhance balance, flexibility, and strength in the body, but the breath work—*pranayama*—and meditation involved (in this case, the practice of remaining nonjudgmentally aware of what our bodies are feeling and doing) result in positive physiological changes as well.[1]

They calm the sympathetic nervous system (which handles our "fight or flight" response) and activate the parasympathetic nervous system (our "rest and digest" functions). Activities such as massage, laughing, meditation, diaphragmatic (or deep belly) breathing, singing/chanting, yoga, and being with friends engage the parasympathetic nervous system. These activities stimulate the vagus nerve, the cranial nerve that is the longest in the autonomic nervous system, passing through the neck to service the heart, lungs, intestinal tract, and back muscles. It sends major neurotransmitters from the brain to the abdomen along what is called the brain-gut axis. Stimulation of the vagus nerve has been found to reduce anxiety, emotional and physical pain, and inflammation in the body, and to increase relaxation, calmness, and positive moods. So mindful yoga practices that stimulate the vagus nerve can serve us well, especially if we can bring them to bear on our difficult conversations.

Reggie Hubbard has stated, "Yoga is a practice of liberation. It is not a practice of comfort." As such, it fosters our ability to respond to discomfort in thoughtful and productive ways. Yoga is also a practice of unity, and the tools we learn through mindfulness and physical practice help us move toward unity rather than discord in relationship with others. This doesn't mean that we will exist in utopia, that we will always agree, or that we will embody perfection. But it does mean that we can learn equanimity, the realization that there is a basic level of calm awareness from which we can consciously choose how to engage with the world. Equanimity has been likened to the awareness that the sky is constant, despite the weather. This metaphor shows us that we, too, can function from the level of our unchanging core self—with its beliefs and values—rather than from the storms of our emotions. The initial challenge is to understand and connect with this deep-rooted self and this deep level of self-awareness. Mindfulness and *asana* (the physical postures) guide us in practicing this awareness because they involve asking deep questions. In the context of talking about race, some of these questions might be:

- When debating with someone who doesn't share my perspective, can I take a breath and, with that breath, expand into recognition of my own safety and the other person's right to differ?
- How am I holding my body? Am I slouching or sitting up straight?
- How am I holding my face?
- Am I ready in this moment to learn? If not, can I accept that reality or can I make adjustments so that I am more ready?
- What am I feeling and how do I process those feelings?
- How can I listen more fully?
- When do I shut down and why?
- How can I open to others' perspectives, thoughts, and experiences?
- Why are these conversations important?
- What do I do to avoid them? Why?
- Do I value another's perspective when it differs from my own? When I don't, what's getting in the way?
- How might I learn to value another perspective more fully?

Part of our practice in mindfulness in difficult conversations is to ask these questions and become nonjudgmentally, compassionately aware of the answers. If the answers point to areas in which we'd like to see growth, our newfound awareness can propel choices toward that growth and positive change. As Asao Inoue encourages: "Let's ask ourselves to pause in our [intellectual] labors and listen to our bodies and recognize that we do writing and reading [all of learning, in fact] in bodies . . . and these bodies matter to the reading and writing and the learning . . . if we pay attention to these things we can learn a lot about our learning, and that's very powerful" (Beals 2020, n.p.). I agree. So ultimately, my answer to the question *Why Be Mindful?* is simple: *we'll reap the benefits, individually and collectively, if we are.*

NOTE

1. For a more comprehensive list of the benefits of *asana*, *pranayama*, and meditation, see appendix C.

Introduction

Where Have We Been? Where Are We Now? Tracing Civil (and Uncivil) Discourse

In 1992, Cornel West wrote an article titled "Let's Talk about Race," and, more recently in 2017, Celeste Headlee wrote *We Need to Talk: How to Have Conversations That Matter*. I, too, have been trying to talk about race and have conversations that matter in university classrooms, where I have taught African American literature and culture and African American/African diaspora studies since 2005. In each class, I engage students with the question of *how* we can have these conversations: What should they entail and, more importantly, how must we be as individuals and communities in order to engage in productive, civil conversations that can be the basis of positive social justice work? This is an essential question for the productivity of each class, and it is an essential question for students to answer as they move beyond the classroom into the world. It's also essential for me as a teacher, specifically as a woman of color in a predominantly white institution. What we each decide in answer to this question can be put into practice in our classrooms and in our larger communities and indeed *should* be—that is, we should be conscious about and prepared (as much as possible) for how we will engage with the differences among us.

There seems to be renewed interest in this topic of civil discourse and its necessity for social justice. As the United States and other countries confront a swell of nationalist sentiment, many people are finding it necessary to talk about *how we talk*: why we must approach each other across differences and how we can do so productively and in a variety of settings—from traditional face-to-face interactions to online settings and social media. Although diversity and inclusion have been long-standing topics of scholarly and institutional attention, more recent discourse also emphasizes both civic engagement and civility in its literal sense—formal politeness and courtesy in behavior or speech. For example, the University of Arizona's National Institute for Civil Discourse (NICD) was created in 2011 and cites a pertinent motivating principle on their website: "People with different values and political preferences can discuss their differences in a civil and productive matter." With programs such as their "Engaging Differences" video series, NICD hopes to encourage viewers to "engage our differences more constructively—to see each other as human beings, not as competing political positions" in a broad-reaching effort to "renew our families, strengthen our neighborhoods, and unite our country, despite our disagreements." These are worthwhile goals at the familial, communal, and national level; they are also necessary goals for the communities we create in our classrooms.

Additionally, these goals can be enhanced strategically through mindfulness practices that help us understand how our emotions fuel our thoughts and therefore our interactions with others. The more conscious we become of our emotional and mental landscape, the more we are able to engage proactively rather than reactively, consciously rather than automatically; in common parlance, we become able to *act* (or not act), rather than *react* in situations with others. Mindfulness practices, therefore, have a place in our preparation for and implementation of challenging conversations. The topics of identity and social justice are "hot" topics, in both senses of the word—they are timely and they are triggers. Productive engagement with these topics demands we remain mindful of how we may be triggered and how we may be triggering others; it demands we pay attention to ourselves at a fundamental level, and it demands that we grant such attention to others. Learning and practicing mindfulness can deeply enhance our conversations and experiences with others, furthering our social justice efforts at their most basic stage: person to person.

This book takes a holistic approach to the classroom and the people within it, recognizing and prioritizing what I call whole people and whole conversations—that is, those that acknowledge students and teachers as more than just talking heads, intellectuals in exchange. Rather, seeing people *wholly* foregrounds their physical, intellectual, and emotional selves. In this light, we can hear the words of a heated argument while we also feel the primal responses of anger and/or fear—the loud or trembling voice, the flush of sweat, the clenched fists and defensive postures. Through recognizing these in ourselves and others, we can begin to make conscious decisions about how we will continue in conversation with and relationship to others. Similarly, whole conversations prioritize people *as people*, rather than as political ideologies or social standing, and encourage listening over dominating, being heard over winning. In other words, such conversations aim to foster understanding and common ground rather than argumentation. They aim for dialogue rather than debate.

The Mindful Classroom focuses on race, identity, and social justice in particular because these remain core topics of civic life, as they have been for centuries, and they have again risen to higher levels in popular consciousness in recent years. In 2012, Trayvon Martin was shot and killed by George Zimmerman, who in 2013 was acquitted of murder. The acquittal prompted the creation of #BlackLivesMatter on social media, and Black Lives Matter was born as a movement to bring awareness of police brutality and state-sanctioned violence against black people and to demand institutional-level change. In 2014, Michael Brown, Jr. was murdered in Ferguson, Missouri, garnering worldwide attention. Sandra Bland was killed in 2015. That same year #SayHerName was created to raise awareness of black female victims of police violence and antiblack violence in the United States, with victims including Eric Garner, Tamir Rice, Walter Scott, Philando Castile, George Floyd, Ahmaud Arbery, and Breonna Taylor. We know the list is despairingly long. Cell phones that capture video and social media have allowed much broader awareness of racism and the lived realities of minorities in the United States. These realities are not solely oppressive, to be sure, but the fact that they are oppressive at all demands our attention and national intervention. The murder of George Floyd was so egregious that no one could deny the excessive use of force by his murderer or the callous disregard for human life by surrounding officers.[1] The deliberate racialized power and privilege of a white woman in the case of black birdwatcher Christian Cooper also highlighted white supremacy as an often-conscious force wielded by white people in order to contain, suppress, and punish people of color as they go about the business of being human.

The world is aware. And while there are those who attempt to deny, justify, or cry reverse racism, many more are awakening and becoming "woke." They are actively working to be anti-racist, and the conversations on how to be so are widespread. For years, there has been burgeoning interest in "diversity and inclusion topics," and there is a resurgence of interest in civility, civil discourse, and inclusive conversations since the 2016 U.S. presidential election. With widespread public attention again turned to racial injustice, new anti-racism statements are being crafted and anti-racist actions are being exercised. At my university, new task forces abound as we work to create anti-racist curricula, to promote anti-racist faculty development, to support minority student, staff, and faculty recruitment and retention, and to assist in consciousness raising. At my local yoga studio, we hold "racial roundtables" where white people and people of color engage with these topics on an interpersonal level. These conversations are necessary. And they are hard.

My intention with this book is to acknowledge both the necessity and difficulty of these conversations. They are necessary because things must change, and as Margaret J. Wheatley reminds us, "All social change begins with a conversation" (Wheatley 2002, n.p.). Our conversations must lead to action, but we often need help negotiating these conversations. This book is designed to help all of us in these conversations through mindfulness and yoga practices. Whether we are educators, students, facilitators, or community members, we who participate in these conversations are people who must be recognized in all our complexity. We feel emotions. We have minds that run away from us. We tense our bodies. We clench our fists. We forget to breathe. We exist in bodies that are seen in certain, sometimes predetermined ways, yet we are unique individuals with intersectional identities that belie stereotypes.

ENGAGING IDENTITY

Despite the ongoing critiques of identity politics, it is important to recognize the saliency of identity in individual lives (significantly so in traditional college-aged populations, as late adolescence remains a time of critical self-inquiry and discovery). And, although identity is often prioritized individually, critiques of identity politics show us that identity needn't be the sun around which our social justice planets revolve. Additionally, race remains a crucial lens through which we engage difference and a notoriously difficult topic to talk about. As Derald Wing Sue has noted, dialogues on race "inevitably evoke a clash of racial realities" (Sue 2015, 6) when the participants are from different racial groups. Because race is such a central component of many people's identities—whether they are conscious of this fact or not—individuals must equip themselves to understand its social functions and effects, discuss its constructions and manifestations, and openly consider its results at both individual and collective levels.

Although Eastern practices acknowledge the interconnectedness of all lives, they also acknowledge that we go about our daily lives individually—with differing bodies, experiences, upbringings and activities. Of course, this awareness of connection is not limited to Eastern traditions. Martin Luther King, Jr.—drawing from the wisdom of Mohandas Gandhi—famously spoke of beloved community, acknowledging: "all life is interrelated" and we exist "in an inescapable network of mutuality, tied in a single garment of destiny. Whatever affects one directly, affects all indirectly" (quoted in Johnson 2014, 34). Awareness of shared humanity and the ways in which our lives are intertwined and mutually determinant spans the globe. This awareness recognizes the particular in the universal, as well as how the particular can divide us from the universal. As Charles Johnson notes, awareness of America's racial structures allows people to see many Eurocentric whites project fictitious racial "substance" (or meaning) onto people of color, never seeing the mutable individual before them. (Just as unenlightened men do with women.) In their thinking, they dualistically carve the world up in terms of the illusory constructs of "whiteness" and "blackness" and, on the basis of this mental projection, create social structures . . . that fuel attachment, clinging, prejudice, and what the Dharma describes as the "three poisons" of ignorance, hatred, and greed. (Johnson 2014, 29)

Nevertheless, these particulars can also help us acknowledge and address injustices that we and others face: while we need not be "*blind* to what [our] own valuable yet adventitious racial, gender, or class differences reveal to [us], neither [are we] *bound* by them; and those very phenomenal conditions may, in fact, spark [our] dedication to social transformations intended to help all sentient beings achieve liberation" (Johnson 2014, 30). These particulars of identity are touchstones for conversations about society and its ills, conversations from which we can launch our efforts toward universal social justice.

As a certified yoga teacher, I have been teaching the physical and mental practices of yoga and meditation since 2007. I have taught countless classes and workshops in yoga studios, churches, and health centers and have also incorporated yoga and meditation into a number of my literature and community-based learning classes at the university level. Additionally, I have taught literature classes on Eastern philosophy and empathy. As a race studies scholar and teacher, I have seen how the incorporation of yoga, meditation, and mindfulness techniques have opened up wider spaces for dialogue on challenging topics. I have seen in myself and others how mindfulness and stress-reducing practices help alleviate much of the anxiety involved in difficult conversations and engagements of difference. I aim for this book to make such practices accessible—and acceptable—for others' classrooms and conversations as well.

The Mindful Classroom is a book on "teaching and talking race," blending pedagogical theory, race theory, yoga exercises, mindfulness and yoga practices, Eastern philosophy, and student reflection. I hope it will be of use to students, scholars, and teachers of race studies, cultural studies, civility studies, pedagogical theory and practice, deliberative pedagogy, and social justice. The work will also be of interest to teachers of community-based learning and community engagement courses; professionals who work in community organizing; and facilitators of discussions on race, diversity, and inclusivity. In terms of student use, it will be most appropriate for those at the graduate level who are studying teaching methodologies and practices. Additionally, this work will be valuable for those in traditional classrooms as well as online settings. Since it specifically includes information on fostering civil conversations online, it is pertinent in the wake of the COVID-19 pandemic, when more classes and conversations have moved online.

This work fits within a growing collection of scholarly work attending to civil discourse, deliberative pedagogy, social justice, and pedagogy. It also links with work that engages the teaching of race-based topics and with burgeoning interest in mindfulness and pedagogy.

For example, *Race & Pedagogy: Creating Collaborative Spaces for Teacher Transformations* by Susan R. Adams and Jamie Buffington-Adams aims to help teachers confront implicit bias. *Race & Pedagogy* challenges them to discuss their own experiences and backgrounds in order to confront the failings of the educational system.

In their highly data-driven book *Social Justice Issues & Racism in the College Classroom*, Dannielle Joy Davis and Patricia G. Bower use both quantitative and qualitative research to explore the topic of race and social justice in college classrooms. Drawing mainly on minority perspectives, the book highlights how faculty and students of color approach the issues of race, social justice, and academic marginalization, although attention is also given to how nonminority faculty and students can support people of color.

In *Race Dialogues: A Facilitator's Guide to Tackling the Elephant in the Classroom*, Donna Rich Kaplowitch et al. do an excellent job of presenting the challenges that accompany race-based discussions in high school and college classrooms as well as in other learning communities. Acknowledging the difficult emotions that often fill such conversations, the authors share best practices for facilitation via lesson plans and other materials. With its focus on participatory democracy and diverse-group dialogue, the book details topics such as inclusivity, asking good questions, multiple ways of knowing, dealing with conflict, and managing resistance.

As a clear-headed guide to teaching, Cyndi Kernahan's book *Teaching about Race: Race and Racism in the College Classroom: Notes from a White Professor* acknowledges the strong emotions that accompany conversations on race. Knowing that teachers can lead these honest yet painful conversations, the book also reminds teachers of ways to make such discussions compassionate and student-centered. Helpfully, it considers differences between teacher and student responses to race as well as common differences in the responses of white students and students of color. Additionally, it provides a practical chapter on course content, problems, and solutions.

In *The Emperor Has No Clothes: Teaching about Race & Racism to People Who Don't Want to Know*, Tema Okun provides a useful pedagogically based text for educators who are interested in classroom conversations about race and oppression. Most interesting is its attention to teaching people past their conditioned fear-based responses and its conclusion that collaborative action is a fundamental outcome of such teaching. In terms of theory, the book covers topics such as binary thinking, denial, and the construction of hegemony.

Karen Ragoonaden has edited a cross-disciplinary and evidence-based collection entitled *Mindful Teaching and Learning: Developing a Pedagogy of Well-Being*. Geared toward teacher education, it is useful for teachers who are interested in student well-being, holistic lesson planning, and mindfulness literacy.

Race Talk and the Conspiracy of Silence: Understanding and Facilitating Difficult Dialogues on Race by Derald Wing Sue is also an excellent resource for those facilitating conversations on race. As a sequel to *Microaggressions in Everyday Life*, the book defines race talk and offers practical guidelines for how to facilitate it. It explores the differences between "white talk" and "black talk" and considers why talking about race is often a challenging task for both white people and people of color.

Finally, in their collection *Race in the College Classroom: Pedagogy and Politics*, Bonnie TuSmith and Maureen T. Reddy include chapters that focus specifically on race as a subject within college classrooms. The collection deals with questions such as authority and legitimacy, challenges in confronting race-based issues, and transformative practices. With its social justice basis, it discusses the rewards and pitfalls of tackling the issue of race among varied populations of college students.

The Mindful Classroom extends this tradition in scholarship and joins the strands of mindfulness; pedagogy; and race, identity, and social justice. This book is meant to answer "why?" and "how?"—why should we engage in mindfulness practices (especially in challenging conversations about race, identity, and social justice) and how we can do so. It begins in chapter 1 with a discussion of race and its meanings, especially in terms of individual identity, personal agency, and collective struggles toward social justice. Chapter 2 addresses how we can create constructive conversations and communities, both face-to-face and online. In chapter 3, I draw from my background in literary studies to consider how literature can help foster empathy and build our practices for engaging with difference in the world. Similarly, Chapter 4 features insights from community-based learning theories and practices to help individuals take their classroom-based practices into engagement with people in surrounding communities.

Diverging from the theory- and practice-based discussions of the previous chapters, chapters 5 offers models for creating syllabi, community-based learning projects, assignments, and rubrics that foster constructive conversations on race, identity, and justice. Many of these can be used across platforms, meaning they are relevant whether the conversations are face-to-face or online. Chapter 6 highlights the voices of engaged students in their reflections on applying mindfulness or community engagement to their classroom and daily experiences. Because this book seeks to foster constructive conversations among student/teacher populations, it is worthwhile to consider student perspectives on the importance and difficulty of these conversations. What has worked for students in their engagements with difference? How has mindfulness fostered their conversations within the classroom and beyond it (even online and in social media)? What new knowledge are they creating via mindful conversations, and how does this knowledge impact their lives outside the classroom? How do they plan to use what they know? How have they already used this new knowledge (either in community-based learning settings or in their daily lives)? Student reflection on these and other questions can aid teachers as they plan classes and classroom dialogue, helping teachers foster mindful classrooms where students feel safe enough to make themselves wholly present.

In the conclusion, I consider where we might go from here, asking what the communities to come might look like if more widespread engagement with mindfulness practices ensues. Finally, an afterword is offered by Andrew Woods, a former student of mine who understands the importance of moving from classroom conversations to real-world commitment toward social justice. The appendices offer important definitions for conversations on race and justice; tips for intervening in racist conversations; and a list of resources and organizations dedicated to mindfulness practices and yoga, self-care, and somatics; holistic teaching; discussion facilitation; and social justice, including countering bias and hate and being an ally.

Also interspersed throughout the book are four "Mindfulness and Movement Practices" following each of the chapters from 1 to 4. These sections are designed around the body-mind-spirit triad that is discussed in holistic health and wellness circles, including those of yoga and meditation. "The Body" exercises offer physical practices, including alternatives for those who have physical disabilities; "The Mind" exercises include meditations; and "The Spirit" exercises focus on breath work (*pranayama*). Each of these can be performed as a group in a classroom or conference room—whether those rooms are face-to-face or virtual—or they can be practiced individually. At the end of each of these sections, I also offer suggestions for less formalized versions of these practices that can be engaged in everyday life to enhance mindful, nonjudgmental awareness of the present moment. Here and in each section, I also remind facilitators to be very cautious when sharing movement exercises with a class, especially if facilitators do not have formal training. Although the practices are typically non-strenuous and although I offer suggestions for modifications, students with back, neck, or other physical challenges could hurt themselves. It is crucial that students listen to the prompts of their own bodies, letting their personal awareness override any suggestions that come from the facilitator that might cause pain. I advise facilitators to emphasize Mind and Breath work and with the Body to suggest small, more readily available movements—such as wrist circles or shoulder rolls—that are more likely to be accessible for a wide group of practitioners.

I recognize how unusual it will be for most classroom educators or discussion facilitators in business settings to interrupt active thinking and talking in order to focus on body movements or meditative exercises. However, if we introduce students to our classes with the understanding that we will consistently guide them in mindfulness and movement exercises at the beginning or end of each class, we will establish a classroom culture where such practices are normalized and even welcomed. Encouraging movements as common as wrist and ankle circles, shoulder rolls, and swaying side to side can help focus minds and release tension in the body as students enter class and prepare for conversation; you might think of these like warm-ups before a game. Then, if we need to interrupt an unproductive conversation with these or more involved exercises, students will likely feel less resistance to them. And we might take a cue from elementary school teachers who know more immediately the importance of discharging energy from the body in order to focus the mind. Although most of us are aware of the role body language plays in communication, protocol has dictated that adults focus most of their attention away from their bodies in professional and academic settings. We would do well to recognize the ways our bodies not only communicate our feelings to others but the ways they can communicate to us as well, if we're mindful enough to listen. Recognizing, managing, and releasing tension in the body can help us refocus our minds—and our thoughts can give us clues to our emotional and mental state, which we can then direct more consciously.

As my wise colleague Chris Janson says, "The process of teaching is as valuable as the content."[2] So, too, is the process of mindfulness, a continually enacted practice that reveals to us much more than the content of our thoughts. It reveals our habits and patterns (of body, mind, and emotion) and our preconditioned responses and limitations, moving us closer to an inner freedom that can guide our liberation efforts for all.

NOTES

1. I greatly appreciate the work of Resmaa Menakem, especially his book *My Grandmother's Hands: Racialized Trauma and the Pathway to Mending Our Hearts and Bodies*. Although I never condone murder or police brutality, Menakem's work helps me recognize police officers not just as entities within a larger system of systemic racism but also as embodied individuals who carry race-based traumas in their bodies. This trauma, like that in every person, is "all about speed and reflexivity" and can trigger mindless reaction if not mindfully addressed and healed (26).

2. Chris Janson, email to author, January 23, 2017.

Chapter 1

What We Talk about When We Talk about Race

Encountering Individual Identity, Personal Agency, and Collective Struggle

At the university where I work, I have regularly taught a class called Black American Literature. Given its name, the class is populated by students who know we'll be talking about race, black American culture, and literature. But that doesn't mean that every student already knows what race is or productive ways to talk about it. Black students who take the class typically are more familiar with these conversations, but because the university is a predominantly white institution, there are always students present who have less familiarity with discussions about race. They might feel curiosity, anger (at racial injustice or challenges to white privilege), frustration, or outright discomfort. As Robin DiAngelo writes in *White Fragility: Why It's So Hard for White People to Talk about Racism*, "when we try to talk openly and honestly about race, white fragility quickly emerges as we are so often met with silence, defensiveness, argumentation, certitude, and other forms of pushback" (DiAngelo 2018, 8). Such discomfort is not the exclusive purview of the white students in the class; minority students often feel frustration, anger, and discomfort too (though not motivated by the same sources), as do I—despite having facilitated conversations on race for over two decades.

Race often makes people uncomfortable because it is one of those components on which identities have been built—whether we're conscious of that fact or not. People have worn race like an invisible badge or a solid burden, like a chip on their shoulders or an albatross around their necks. It's been a mark of shame, a scarlet letter, a source of confusion and blame. For others, it's been carried like a rite of passage, like warrior marks, like an admired or a shameful tattoo. And race has been a question: *What is this really, and how does it shape who I am?*

This question of *Who am I?* is far from unique and in the realm of race studies has provided the basis for countless explorations in sociology, literature, culture, and life. Several years ago, this question was made explicit at my institution with the visit of the Human Race Experience, a photo booth that uses software to "re-racialize" a snapshot of a person. The kiosk's purpose was to help us imagine who we would be if we looked different. It's a strange concept, especially when we recognize the vast phenotypical differences of people within a racial group. In reality, it was a superficial exercise, even a trivializing game, because we cannot simply try on and then discard a different race. We can't have a truly racialized experience from standing within the safety of a kiosk. As my English department colleague Kelsi Hasden expressed, "There is a long history of this action, of 'trying on' and discarding other races" in blackface minstrel shows, for example, or in the history of passing—again, stemming from vastly different motivations.[1] The scholarship on these practices is rich, and we should certainly be diligent about not letting experiences such as that touted by the Human Race Experience slip shamefully into insult and mockery on the one hand, escape or even shallow entertainment on the other. Instead, we must respond more deeply to such exercises, including those within classroom settings, first taking the opportunity to interrogate racial identity itself and second, moving from playing with the idea of identity to solid work for social justice, making real movements toward anti-racism. I'll begin with a discussion of the former in hopes of leading clearly to the latter.

If we follow the "Who am I" question farther, we might ask *what does how I look have to do with who I am?* And *how would looking different than I do change my path through the world?* Or, conversely, *how is it that the way I look now has been determinant of my life experiences?* These are standard questions for most visible racial minorities, although historically they have been less fully explored by the majority (so the Human Race Experience was likely more edifying for them).

In any case, these questions point to the fact that identity has been linked to phenotype—to the outward appearance of our bodies—and that our experiences are linked to how others perceive us. If there was any benefit to that Human Race Experience or other experiments like it, I would say it is in recognizing that the questions to which it lends itself point to the phenomenological heart of identity politics: to its suggestion that the identity I have is central to my experience of the world and, by extension, *how I should engage the world.* I hope to explore that premise more fully and, in so doing, contemplate what I among others consider to be the contemporary problem of identity politics.

THE POLITICS OF IDENTITY

Initially, identity politics imagined race as essential and quantifiable. Some people *are* black; others *are* white. These designations might have been made based on phenotype, ancestry, culture, or some other factor. With gender, we can see how this ontological certainty of identity shifted, allowing Simone de Beauvoir to famously remark "One is not *born* but is *made* a woman." Identities may be socially constructed; identities may be performed; but identities in the mid- to late twentieth century often have been the lens through which we see ourselves and the barometer that tells us where our political loyalties should lie.

Civil rights struggles in the 1960s, for example, envisioned black people as a necessary collective, struggling against racist oppression; an identity centered in blackness became a source of solidarity and at times was more important than individual differences within blackness. As Mark Lilla wrote in the *Chronicle of Higher Education*, "Identity politics on the left was at first about large classes of people—African-Americans, women, gays—seeking to redress major historical wrongs by mobilizing and then working through our political institutions to secure their rights" (Lilla 2017, n.p.).

Later, the conversation turned to the heterogeneity within a given identity group (e.g., African Americans) and efforts were made to eliminate oppressions within the community (e.g., based on gender, class, and sexuality). We've also engaged more thoroughly with intersectionality within identity, the idea that our various identities overlap and influence each other in unique ways. Developed by Kimberlé Crenshaw, intersectionality theory explores how our various identities interact with each other to produce unique identities that are met by unique oppressions. Although Crenshaw affirms in "Mapping the Margins" that identity politics can be useful—"recognizing that identity politics takes place at the site where categories intersect thus seems more fruitful than challenging the possibility of talking about categories at all" (Crenshaw 1991, 1299)—identity politics can also divide communities, as groups may articulate (very real and undeniable) differences and forgo uniting beyond those differences against common oppressions. As Lilla plainly puts it, "By the 1980s [identity politics] had given way to a pseudo-politics of self-regard and increasingly narrow and exclusionary self-definition. . . . The main result has been to turn young people back onto themselves, rather than turning them outward toward the wider world they share with others." He goes on to claim that this trend has left people "unprepared to think about *the common good in non-identity terms* and what must be done practically to secure it—especially the hard and unglamorous task of persuading people very different from themselves to join a common effort," which is part of the work of civil discourse, deliberative pedagogy, and social justice (Lilla 2017, n.p.). "Every advance of liberal *identity* consciousness," he writes, "has marked a retreat of effective liberal *political* consciousness" (italics mine). In other words, we have largely lost "a sense of what we share as citizens and what binds us as a nation" (Lilla 2017, n.p.).

So this leads me to ask yet another question: What does this mean for the democratic politics of identity politics? Mark Lilla gives an answer to this question. He writes: "The experience of [the 1960s] taught the New Left two lessons. The first was that movement politics was the only mode of engagement that actually changes things (which once was true but no longer is). The second was that political activity must have some authentic meaning for the self, making compromise seem a self-betrayal (which renders ordinary politics impossible)" (Lilla 2017, n.p.).

In the case of race, identity politics maintains historical boundaries that today may be more permeable but ultimately are still in place, which we see ever more fully in contemporary events. White nationalists have fought the removal of Confederate monuments, while liberals recognize that these monuments were not about historical commemoration but about the civil rights era intimidation of black people. We've seen this on university campuses, including the one where I work: students speaking up for black lives and calling for greater diversity and inclusion have been met by some other students with scorn and mocked in racist videos.

Identity politics can function to draw communal boundaries around race, balkanizing what might otherwise be productive political solidarities. Franz Fanon wrote, "I should constantly remind myself that the real *leap* consists in introducing invention into existence. In the world in which I travel, I am endlessly creating myself. And it is by going beyond the historical, instrumental hypothesis that I will initiate my cycle of freedom" (Fanon 1952, 229). Yet, race, as it has been theorized through identity politics (or even as it is toyed with in exercises like the race kiosk), do not, in Fanon's words, "introduce invention into existence." Rather, racial-identity politics are mired in the circularity of signification, and the races referenced are loaded with the weighty connotations of historical baggage. The civil rights movement of the 1950s and 1960s was an *inter*racial effort toward civil rights—that is, social justice—and was concerned with fostering Martin Luther King, Jr.'s notion of beloved community, a community he explicitly populated beyond the markers of race and identity in his "I Have a Dream" speech. Yet, since the Black Power Movement of the late 1960s and 1970s, most racial discourse has relied on identity politics to articulate struggles against oppression.[2] Henry Louis Gates, Jr. has called race a metaphor for difference; likewise, racial identity becomes a metaphor for myriad aspects of life, ranging from what we call culture to presumed *racialized* experiences.[3] And one of the failures of identity politics is that it takes this metaphor of race as paramount, forgetting the actual signified (people who need freedom from oppression) in favor of the signifier (black man, black woman, Chicano/a, lesbian, etc.). The supposition here is based on synecdoche; the signifier of race comes to stand in for the whole person, allowing us to imagine that who we are *is* our skin color or our ancestry or our gender.[4] Thus, in the words of Jill Olumide, "the challenge is to promote fairness and absence of discrimination by means other than racially divided statistics" (Olumide 2002, 154); in other words, to attempt a move beyond the metaphors in our efforts toward social justice.[5]

Identity has been the fuel that has moved most social justice efforts since the civil rights movement. For example, Trey Ellis's discussion of "The New Black Aesthetic," originally published in 1989, relied on an early articulation of "Post-Black" identity to articulate a new aesthetic among young black people. The aesthetic, he said, "shamelessly borrows and reassembles across both race and class lines" (Ellis 2003, 187). Ellis highlighted the cross-pollination that occurs within this New Black Aesthetic by drawing a parallel between race mixture and cultural bricolage. He wrote, "Just as a genetic mulatto is a black person of mixed parents who can often get along fine with his white grandparents, a cultural mulatto, educated by a multi-racial mix of cultures, can also navigate easily in the white world" (Ellis 2003, 189). Ellis's comment, of course, and his use of the archaic biologically rooted term "mulatto" drew his argument dangerously close to biological understandings of race.

Ellis relied on this trope of race mixture in attempting to broaden understandings of blackness, yet these understandings, too, relied on essentializations of blackness even in the attempt to expand it. He stated, "I, along with the battalions of other young black artists I run into . . . all grew up feeling misunderstood by both the black world and the white. Alienated (junior) intellectuals, we are the more and more young blacks getting back into jazz and the blues; the only ones you see at punk concerts; the ones in the bookstore wearing little, round glasses and short, nat dreads; some of the only blacks who admit liking both Jim and Toni Morrison" (Ellis 2003, 186). Defending an interest in Jim Morrison and punk music as acceptable within blackness was necessary only because races have remained in the realm of the disparate and discrete, and his defense was made through reversions to otherwise obsolete notions of race—that is, that race is essential, even biological. Believing "blackness" can be contradicted by behavior means blackness itself is fixed by historical stereotype.

We have seen a shift in identity politics through postmodern efforts such as Ellis's to deconstruct identities and show them as various, heterogeneous and multiplicitous. However, despite this attempt to expand the meaning of racial identity, the central problem has remained: racial identity cannot be expanded enough so that it no longer divides or deceives and so that it accurately describes the signified. As a result of these ongoing efforts to make the signifier (identity) representative of the signified (people who experience oppression), attention to articulating and categorizing racial identity has become paramount, and viable political action often effectively has been lost.

Antonia Darder and Rodolfo Torres note this "overwhelming tendency among a variety of critical scholars to focus on the concept of 'race' as a central category of analysis for interpreting the social conditions of inequality and marginalization" (Darder and Torres 1999, 175). Furthermore, they note that this conceptualization of race has "reinforced a racialized politics of identity and representation, with its problematic emphasis on 'racial' identity as the overwhelming impulse for political action" (Darder and Torres 1999, 175). Darder and Torres conclude that "the theories, practices, and policies that have informed social science analysis of racialized populations today are overwhelmingly rooted in a politics of identity, an approach that is founded on parochial notions of 'race' and representation which [at times] ignore the imperatives of capitalist accumulation and the existence of class divisions within racialized subordinate populations" (Darder and Torres 1999, 175). Although many have been effective in articulating the lived dilemmas *individuals* face in describing their experiences and finding communities of belonging, the focus on identity, like the race kiosk, does not offer enough of an attendant focus on changes in social structures, institutions, and policies that maintain oppression.

I am not claiming that new representations of lived experiences are not useful; rather, I am suggesting that attention to representing these experiences, encouraged by contemporary identity politics, highlights only one factor: racial identity. Although these efforts hope to forge new communities, they seem to do so only by over-determining the individual. The focus on individualized difference often presupposes and even creates divisions among other communities. Likewise, this focus often comes at the expense of challenging the larger social structures that maintain *collective, material* realities of oppression.

Because of this, we might be more mindful in our uses of identity politics, which have prioritized identity *at the expense of* politics; identity politics has turned political solidarity into inexhaustible divisions based on signifiers. And this attention to signification—revealed in the prioritizing of racial identity—has distracted us from a more progressive politics against racism for the twenty-first century. As Fanon urges us to remember, it will be through movements *beyond* these earlier racial tropes and ideologies, including those of race-based identity politics, that we will free ourselves from the struggles that race as we know it has necessitated and maintained. Moving beyond the snare of racialized identity politics may allow us to rethink ourselves, our communities, and our struggles against oppression.

What I find heartening in terms of some contemporary politics is a growing recognition and return to the fact that we cannot be silent about others' oppressions. We are seeing alliances that are reminiscent of the strong Jewish involvement in and support of the civil rights movement. We are seeing white people claim their responsibility to be "white and woke," cis-gender people claim their responsibility to be allies for LGBTQ+ people, "temporarily able-bodied" people (to use my colleague Brandy Winfrey's term) claim their responsibility to work for the rights of people with disabilities. And *on* the list must go.

Here, I can return to Mark Lilla and the role of education in fostering politics beyond identity politics. Lilla writes about contemporary liberal pedagogy and its common focus on identity, claiming it is "actually a depoliticizing force. It has made our children more tolerant of others than [earlier generations were], which is a very good thing. But by undermining the universal democratic *we* on which solidarity can be built, duty instilled, and action inspired, it is unmaking rather than making citizens. In the end this approach just strengthens all the atomizing forces that dominate our age" (Lilla 2017, n.p.).

He reminds us that there is something to be said for higher education before the late 1960s (despite its clear faults), that *pre-identity-focused* education that produced the likes of Elizabeth Cady Stanton (who studied Greek) and Martin Luther King, Jr. (who studied Christian theology) and Angela Davis (who studied Western philosophy). Don't misunderstand me, there is clear value in African American studies, in disability studies, in reading Native American and women's literature, especially for those who don't hold those identities. There is necessary value in education that takes people beyond their individual identities and experiences and that fosters, again in Lilla's words, "passion and commitment, but also knowledge and argument. Curiosity about the world outside your own head and about people unlike yourself. Care for this country and its citizens, all of them, and a willingness to sacrifice for them. And the ambition to imagine a common future for all of us." The most valuable education for our time is an education in human rights and, with it, the understanding that those rights precede—and go far beyond—identity.

MINDFUL OF IDENTITY

To avoid some of the pitfalls in our history of identity politics, we can strive toward more mindful engagements of identity through self-reflection and through turning our attention to the materiality of oppressions and to the experiences of embodied people in the world. In *The Body Is Not an Apology: The Power of Radical Self-Love*, Sonya Renee Taylor reminds us:

When we speak of the ills of the world—violence, poverty, injustice—we are not speaking conceptually; we are talking about things that happen to bodies. When we say millions around the world are impacted by the global epidemic of famine, what we are saying is that millions of humans are experiencing the physical deterioration of muscle and other tissue due to lack of nutrients in their bodies. *Injustice* is an opaque word until we are willing to discuss its material reality. (Taylor 2018, 5)

Here, Taylor shows a way beyond the limitations of identity politics, directing our attention to the basic material realities of oppression and injustice. With these realities in mind, our individually valued identities might become sites of personal agency in collective efforts toward social justice or, at the very least, we might become more conscious of how our individual identities might be used to enhance, rather than hinder, our conversations about race.

This mindful awareness of identity can begin with questions we ask ourselves: "Now why," I [might] wonder, "do I want to believe *that*? Why do I think such a thing [or thought] will bring me happiness? Am I truly seeing this person or thing or feeling clearly? Through my own eyes or those of my parents, friends, teachers or Madison Avenue? Are these thoughts and judgements my own or have I *received* them from others?" (Johnson 2014, 5). In other words, what is the basis of my thinking, even about who and what I am and what I should desire for myself and others? Conscious attention to these questions makes room for mindful answers to arise and mindful responses to ensue, and such investigations into our own interiority is crucial. Johnson also reminds us, quoting from the *Dhammapada*, "Because . . . 'all that we are is the result of what we have thought,' the transformation of 'sociological and psychological structures' must take place initially in our own minds—and those of others—if we truly hope to address the root cause of social suffering" (Johnson 2014, 30).

One assignment I've consistently used in classes that focus on race is the "Who Am I?" personal statement found in chapter 5. Prior to this essay assignment, I usually have the class read Zora Neale Hurston's brief essay "How it Feels to Be Colored Me," which we then discuss as a class. In this essay, Hurston—who grew up in the all-black town of Eatonville, Florida—celebrates herself as an individual, recognizing that a racial identity was placed upon her by white people when she moved to Jacksonville, Florida, to attend school. Subsequently, students are asked to reflect on their understandings and experiences of race, including how they first became aware of it. Even students who have had no race consciousness prior to this assignment are called to reflect on why this would be so. What is it about their upbringing or their social position that has allowed race to *not* be a salient factor in their identities? Since these are personal reflections, students aren't asked to share them with the class, but they often willingly choose to speak from this awareness of the role race has or hasn't played in their understanding of themselves and why.

In my feedback to them, I focus on questions that will deepen students' self-reflections, encouraging them to be ever more mindful of the ways race can function in people's lives or, conversely, how some are allowed to prioritize other parts of their identities. The objective is self-awareness, and with the attendant mindfulness that results, we are usually able to have deepened conversations as a class. Frequently, students refer to their personal statements for examples and anecdotes and for the "ah-ha" moments when they realize how divergent people's experiences of race can be. The fact that these are *personal* statements also highlights the subjectivity of experience and helps to encourage dialogue on those experiences rather than debate about right/wrong belief systems.

I've found this a productive assignment, one that allows students to think critically about identity and its foundations. This, in turn, helps foster further self-reflection as our class discussions progress, encouraging students to interrogate the basis for their identities and their beliefs about race, rather than assume those identities and beliefs are (or should be) universal. This personal assignment paves the way for future "race talk" in the class, and I find it helps students practice more of this mindful reflectiveness as our class discussions move from the personal level to the institutional and systemic.

Attention to the lived realities of bodies in the world and interrogation of their own racial identities are practices that allow students to think more broadly about race and justice. These practices are helpful in allowing expanded awareness of how race is shaped, how racialized experiences are different person to person, and how justice should be a universal *human* concern, not a racial one. Self-reflection assignments are helpful in teaching this content, as are deliberative pedagogy (discussed in chapter 2) and immersions in others' lives—whether that be through the empathic imagination (discussed in chapter 3) or community-engaged learning (discussed in chapter 4). These pedagogical models help move students away from the divisiveness of identity politics and into a space where their individual identity can be enacted on behalf of others. Those who identify particular privileges allowed by their identities can inhabit those spaces with a mind toward helping those who don't have those privileges reach a common level of justice. For example, in appendix A, I discuss how those within a racial group can intervene when they hear others in their group engage in racist conversations.

Similarly, fostering mindfulness about students' own foundations—their beliefs, feelings, attitudes—can help them begin to see how these foundations shape not only their perspectives but also their actions. The mindfulness practices suggested throughout this book help foster this awareness, which comes with an attendant understanding that students can choose to retain or discard some of these foundations. Empowering students with the awareness and autonomous choice of their core beliefs is one of the most important lessons of education. From this awareness and conscious choice, students can direct themselves on how they wish to enact their identities and exist in relationship with others.

BRINGING MINDFUL RACE TALK INTO THE CLASSROOM

After attending to the basis for students' personal identities and the foundations for their beliefs about race, conversation can move toward more challenging race talk[6]—those conversations that focus on race, racism, and privilege. According to Borsheim-Black and Sarigianides, "One of the central goals of racial literacy is to be able to engage in race talk, even when it is hard and uncomfortable to do so" (Borsheim-Black and Sarigianides 2019, 88). In their chapter "Planning for and Responding to Race Talk," the authors discuss common challenges in engaging students in race talk in college classrooms, particularly white students who have been taught that "*not* talking about race and racism [is] polite and politic . . . while calling attention to those subjects can be perceived as a racist act" (Borsheim-Black and Sarigianides 2019, 91). I find it helpful to discuss this issue early on, letting students know that our conversations will move past colorblindness and into the realm of the uncomfortable. Students need to know that they are being asked to be comfortable with allowing discomfort. Crucially, I also let students know that what is uncomfortable needn't feel dangerous or unsafe— though foundational beliefs may be challenged in our conversations, the aim of those conversations is awareness and broadened perspectives not attack or annihilation. Growth necessitates discomfort. In yoga, for instance, we learn to distinguish dull and achy *discomfort* from sharp and electrical *pain*. The former is uncomfortable. The latter is dangerous and unsafe. The former we sit with, we feel and experience, and we often note that the dull, achy discomfort begins to shift as we allow our bodies to stretch and grow. The latter must be avoided; we must find a new approach to growth that is non-injurious.

It is imperative that discussion facilitators impress upon students the fact that discomfort in these discussions is unavoidable. It is also imperative that facilitators impress upon students that danger and lack of safety are unacceptable. Thus, it is the facilitator's essential work to make sure students understand the difference between discomfort and danger and to equip students with ways to make known any lack of safety they experience so that the facilitator can offer protection.[7]

In academic parlance, we talk about cognitive dissonance—when individuals become aware of contradictory thoughts, beliefs, or values within themselves—as a type of psychological stress. I remind students, though, that such cognitive dissonance is an opportunity for self-awareness and conscious decision making. I assure them that the growth issuing out of our conversations isn't necessarily a change in mindset but an opportunity for them to understand their own minds—and those of others'—more fully. In this way, they can make more conscious choices about their beliefs and, subsequently, their actions. In other words, they can have personal agency for their own lives. I'm explicit about the fact that my job as a teacher—a discussion facilitator—is to encourage their honest reflection and their open-mindedness through questions. Often, I share with them a paraphrase from Alice Walker's novel *Meridian*: "I imagine good teaching as a circle of earnest people gathered to ask meaningful questions, not as a handing down of answers."

In addressing these often unconscious beliefs and fears students may have, I'm calling on them and myself to be mindful in our classroom engagements with each other and with the ideas we'll be circulating. I'm also encouraging their brave participation by reassuring them of the aim of these conversations: we're not embarking on a battle but an excursion into the depths of ourselves and those in our community. *This* is the adventure of learning.

Having set this stage for mindful engagement in our conversations, I've covered some of what Borsheim-Black and Sarigianides call "proactive strategies" (Borsheim-Black and Sarigianides 2019, 94).[8] Even with this groundwork laid, the class may still find itself in discussions that demand "reactive strategies": "No matter how much we plan or prepare, facilitating race talk presents challenges for even the most experienced teachers" (Borshcim-Black and Sarigianides 2019, 98). We may find the conversation veering off track. We may encounter disengaged students. We may hear "White talk" and "White educational discourse."[9] We may experience heated emotions (discomfort) or outright racist statements (danger) that must be addressed in real time.

Most facilitators are skilled in recognizing and redirecting unproductive paths in conversation. If the conversation is derailing because of white educational discourse, then calling on students to stop and consider the path of the conversation, even to map it together on the chalkboard, can help everyone become mindful of where the conversation is going but perhaps even what emotions are at play when we attempt to avoid or defend against a certain topic. The mindfulness and movement practices following this chapter also can help students become aware of emotional triggers and refocus the mind. Even clearing physical restlessness, which can be a sign of emotional and mental uneasiness, can help students—and the conversation—recenter. Journaling exercises or meditation practices can help disengaged students find the root causes of their disengagement or, as I discuss in chapter 5, visual rather than verbal responses to topics may help certain students feel more engaged. All of these options can help the facilitator as well, especially in an encounter with racist speech, when the moment demands swift but calm attention. A facilitator who is able to witness emotional responses in themselves and others and then respond from a place of mental clarity will have more success in combating racism, supporting students who have been victimized, and setting boundaries to ensure a safer space for productive conversations in the future.

LET'S TALK

As facilitators, we might also encounter resistance from students who don't see the point of having these conversations at all. In these instances, we can remind students of the usefulness of dialogue for broadening our perspectives—a key component of learning—and we can emphasize the value of diverse viewpoints—a key reality of community building as well as a much-desired skill in business. Learning and community building are primary functions in the classroom and also the topics of chapter 2, which focuses on creating constructive conversations and communities.

NOTES

1. Kelsi Hasden, email to author, October 9, 2017.

2. I distinguish Black Nationalist Movements (one during the early 1900s and one during the late 1960s and 1970s) as having centralized identity politics because they prioritized a redefinition and elevation of blackness as a distinct and separate identity as a necessary means to end oppression. Articulating slogans such as "Say it loud, I'm black and proud" and "Black is beautiful," the Black Power Movement of the mid-twentieth century was clearly concerned with reenvisioning the racial identity of blackness in addition to securing political rights. Other movements—for example, the Chicano Movement, the Feminist Movement, and the Black Feminist Movement—have followed suit in highlighting disparate identities and using these identities to gain political power.

3. The troublesome circularity of this definition is already apparent.

4. Indeed, we allow our identities to become synonymous with many other signifiers, even our jobs, the cars we drive, the brand of jeans we wear, the neighborhoods we live in, the country of our birth, and so on.

5. I recognize the practical difficulty of accomplishing this since oppressions themselves are enacted on the bases of racialized divisions.

6. Derald Wing Sue discusses this term in *Race Talk and the Conspiracy of Silence: Understanding and Facilitating Difficult Dialogues on Race.*

7. In chapter 5, I offer practical ways to foster safety for participants in these conversations.

8. I address more proactive strategies for creating constructive conversations in chapter 2.

9. White educational discourse (Haviland) defines common responses white people offer in predominantly white settings that allow them to circumvent, challenge, and even subvert constructive conversations on race. Borsheim-Black and Sarigianides document these thoroughly—from using avoiding words and asserting ignorance or uncertainty to joking, affirming sameness, and sharing personal information (2019, 96).

Mindfulness and Movement Practices

HUMAN BEINGS

You have probably heard the saying, "We are human beings, not human doings," reminding us that we spend so much of our lives doing, often without taking the time to simply be. In "being" we slow down, find stillness, and learn about ourselves more fully. In being, we can ask the questions *Who am I? What do I want? What is my purpose?* And we can observe the answers that arise, typically more honestly because they come from a deeper place than our conscious thoughts, troubled as they can be by our material desires, others' expectations, and our own doubts and fears of what's possible.

In meditation traditions, there is a distinction made between the thinking mind and the observing mind. The thinking mind handles our processes of analysis, planning, and narrating. The observing mind, in contrast, watches. This is the "witness" we hear described in meditation classes. The observing mind witnesses without judgment, expectation, or storytelling. It sees our desire to fidget during a seated meditation but doesn't tell us: *You're doing it wrong! When will you settle down?!* Or, as one meditation teacher shared with me recently, my observing mind sees that I have a flat tire, knows that I will be late for a meeting, and then proceeds to address the needs of the moment: fixing the flat tire. The thinking mind creates a story out of my lateness; it frets and produces anxiety; it causes me to lose focus on what I need to accomplish in the moment. The observing mind is aware of the facts but doesn't dwell on an emotional response or story. It accepts the situation as it is, allowing "discriminating wisdom on how to proceed."[1] The following mindfulness and movement practices are designed to help us tap into this "discriminating wisdom" of the observing mind.

*BODY

Note: Always use extreme caution when beginning or facilitating a new movement practice. Practitioners may be advised to consult a medical professional or trained movement specialist before attempting specific body-based practices. Facilitators should remind practitioners that they must not move in any way that will be injurious or cause pain.

Six Movements of the Spine

In yogic traditions, youthfulness has been tied to the flexibility of the spine. Keeping the spine flexible opens up the neurological pathway from the brain that signals every other part of the body. When our spine is flexible, we can feel increased energy and youthfulness in the body and a sharpened focus in the mind. The spine has three planes of movement—side to side, front to back, and twisting in each direction—resulting in six movements of the spine.

To Practice

You can be seated or standing; alternatively, it can be practiced on hands and knees in tabletop position.

1. Linking movement with breath, inhale and expand the chest forward while taking the shoulders back, the head (or the gaze) up, and the pelvis back. On hands and knees, the belly will sink toward the ground in what is called "cow pose." If it feels painful in the neck to lift the head in this position, then leave the neck neutral, in line with the rest of the spine.
2. Exhaling, round the spine back while the shoulders round forward, the head (or gaze) moves down, and the pelvis moves forward. On hands and knees, you will feel like a cat arching its back, rounding its tail under—"cat pose."
3. Repeat this movement for several sets of inhalations and exhalations before moving on to the next movement.
4. If seated or standing, extend the right arm upward while keeping the shoulder rooted in its socket. On an exhale the arm will curve into a long crescent shape above the head while the torso curves toward the left. The right hip or foot will remain grounded to the chair or floor. Feel the way this expands the right side of the ribcage, creating space between the intercostal muscles between the ribs. Breathe into this space for several breaths. (If practicing on hands and knees, the hands remain planted while the torso forms a crescent shape to the left and then to the right.)

5. On an inhalation, the torso will return to an upright position. On the following exhalation, return the arm down along the torso. Pause to notice the different sensations on the right side versus the left side of the body.
6. Repeat in the other direction, moving the left arm up and overhead while the torso extends to the right. Remember to link breath with movement.
7. To prepare for the final plane of movement, sit or stand evenly, with both sides of the pelvis or both feet sending equal pressure downward. Inhale to lengthen the spine and then exhale taking the right hand to the left knee or hip while the gaze travels behind you to the left. Breathe here for several sets of breath. On an inhalation, return the torso to center.
8. Repeat in the other direction. (If practicing on hands and knees, keep the hips square and on an exhalation thread the right arm underneath the left armpit, so that the right shoulder and side of the face touch the floor. Breathe several inhalations and exhalations before returning to tabletop position on an inhalation. Repeat on the other side.)

MIND

Body Scan

To Practice

1. Settle into a comfortable position, preferably reclined with the eyes closed. (If seated, make sure the back is fully supported and that the spine is long and extending upward.) Create space between the feet to open the hips, perhaps letting the feet flop open so that the toes are pointing diagonally toward the sides, and rest the arms next to the body with the palms facing up. Alternatively, you can place one hand on your heart and the other on your belly.
2. Become aware of your breath, drawing it deeply into the belly and releasing it fully. Notice the natural flow of the breath, the air coming into the nostrils cooler than the air released on the exhalation. Feel the gentle rise and fall of the belly, the slow lifting and lowering of the chest. Breathing in, affirm "I am here." Breathing out, affirm "I am aware."
3. Shift your awareness to your feet, trying to notice and then release any tension held in the soles of the feet, the tops of the feet, the toes. You might find it helpful to affirm, "My feet relax." Feel them softening and sinking heavily toward the floor.
4. Next, draw your awareness up to your ankles, calves, and shins. Affirm their relaxation as you inhale openness and exhale any tightness or tension, letting gravity give you the sensation of heaviness.

5. Continue this practice of affirming relaxation and releasing tension by drawing your awareness upward, scanning each part of the body for tension: the thighs and hamstrings; the hips and buttocks; the lower, middle, and upper back; the belly and chest; the hands, fingers, and wrists; the forearms and upper arms; the tops and back of the shoulders; the neck and back of the head; the throat and jaw (as the jaw softens, feel the tongue move away from the roof of the mouth, the teeth unclench); the skin around the eyes, ears, and temples (you might imagine the eyes sinking deeper in their sockets); the forehead (feel spaciousness between the eyebrows); and the crown of the head (feel a sensation of openness).
6. As you slowly scan the body, feel it supported by the ground beneath you. You might become aware of a sensation of heaviness as you sink into the floor, or you might feel lightness, as if you were floating above it.
7. If the mind becomes distracted and thoughts try to carry you away, return your attention to the breath and the sensation of relaxation in the body.

Practiced to ultimate relaxation, you might find the conscious mind slipping away while you rest in pure presence. Yogis call this state Yoga Nidra, which is a practice of deep presence and relaxation where the mind rests and one seems to float beyond thought and physical sensation.

When you feel ready, your mind will again become aware of physical presence.

1. Feel the rise and fall of your belly and chest. Inhale "I am here." Exhale "I am aware." Notice any sensations in your body. Notice the state of your mind.
2. Slowly bring movement back: wiggling the fingers and toes, rotating the wrists and ankles. You might find it comforting to roll to one side for a few breaths before pressing up through the hands to come back to a seated position.

Accommodations

Remember that the body scan can be practiced from a seated position (e.g., in a classroom or other group setting) and the duration can be shortened or lengthened depending on the amount of time available. To shorten the practice, simply move more quickly through the various places of the body, rather than skipping over any of them.

SPIRIT

Finding the Breath

To Practice

1. Preferably from a reclined position, place one hand on your chest and one on your belly.
2. Notice which hand rises more.

Many people notice that the hand on the chest moves most, indicating that the breath is focused in the lungs. When we breathe from our lungs, we miss out on the full capacity of our breath to soothe and optimize our nervous systems. Breathing into the belly, diaphragmatic breathing, causes the diaphragm to stimulate the vagus nerve, discussed in the Foreword. Furthermore, with lung breathing, we often fail to utilize our lungs to their full capacity. Like any other part of the body, our lungs are "use it or lose it" organs. When we don't fill them completely, they begin to lose their ability to expand fully. In other words, we contribute to their atrophy and, over time, restrict the amount of oxygen we're able to take into our bodies.

Belly Breathing

To Practice

1. While still reclining, place both hands on the belly and take a deep inhalation, letting the belly rise into the hands.
2. As you exhale, feel the belly release toward the floor. You might imagine pulling your navel toward your spine.
3. As you breathe into and out of the belly several times, try to notice any subtle changes in your mind and body. Do you feel calmer? Are your thoughts racing or are they more quiet? Does your body feel more relaxed or more energized?

Three-Part Breathing

For this practice, you will move the breath from the belly, into the ribcage and finally fully into the lungs. Therefore, the inhalations should be extended, becoming much deeper than before so that you can take in enough air to reach all three parts. This breath exercise can be practiced reclining or seated.

To Practice

1. On a deep inhalation, fill the belly; draw the breath into the ribcage; and then into the lungs. When the breath enters the ribcage, imagine it like the

barrel it is, allowing yourself to extend the ribs out to the sides in addition to in front of the body. If you're seated, you may also recognize the sensation of the ribcage expanding behind you, although this will be harder to access if you are supine. When the breath enters the lungs, recognize that they extend from the bottom of your ribcage to near your collarbone. Thus, to fully fill the lungs, you should draw the breath up into the chest, all the way toward your collarbone. If you're seated, you may even feel the collarbone rise upward.
2. On a long exhalation, release the breath from the top of the lungs downward; then from the ribcage as it draws in toward the spine; and then finally from the belly, moving your navel toward your spine.
3. Practice this for several rounds of breath—moving the inhalations from belly to ribcage to chest and the exhalations from the chest to the ribcage to the belly.
4. Release the breath exercise and return to a more natural but still deep and slow breathing pattern. Notice how you feel in body and mind.

Alternatives

All of the practices I've outlined here can be utilized individually or in groups, face to face or online. For those with physical challenges, seated versions of the exercises may be preferable to standing, supine, or tabletop positions.

CONSTRUCTIVE CONVERSATION APPLICATIONS

Though it would be hard to practice Yoga Nidra in the middle of a classroom conversation, all of the other practices I describe in this section can be undertaken during a pause in difficult conversations—either at the instruction of a teacher or at the internal prompting of a student. If unproductive[2] conflict has arisen or seems imminent, take a moment to deepen and expand the breadth, breathing into the belly to stimulate the vagus nerve. Students might even be asked to stand or sit while engaging the six movements of the spine, which will move pent-up energy and refocus the mind on the body's sensations rather than emotionally triggered responses.

In order for a facilitator to effectively utilize the meditation and movement exercises in a classroom setting, they need to be aware of what is happening with students during a conversation. How do their faces look? How are they holding their bodies? Are their voices sounding louder and more angry, or conversely are they sounding quieter but more forceful and deliberate? Sometimes we won't hear a comment as pointed as, "That's insane! I can't believe you just said that!" Rather, the cues that students are shutting down and not listening are likely to be more subtle. Facilitators' conscious attention to their *own* breath and body patterns will help them recognize tensions that might also be arising in students during a difficult conversation. During these moments, the facilitator can hit "pause" on the conversation, telling students that a practice of breath and body awareness will help everyone see the situation more clearly and then return to the conversation with more productivity.

HUMAN BEINGS DOING: MINDFULNESS IN EVERYDAY LIFE

Throughout the day, take a moment to tune into the breath, recognizing whether you're breathing into belly or lungs and, if the latter, whether your breath could be made deeper and fuller. When driving, sitting at a desk, doing the dishes, or waiting in line, tune into how you're breathing and work to create the breathing pattern that will serve you best in the moment. If you're feeling anxious, for example, try to elongate your exhalations. You might try inhaling for a count of four and exhaling for a count of six. In contrast, if you're needing more energy, then try to lengthen your inhalations, reversing the breath count so that you inhale for six and exhale for four. Notice how you feel and play with how changing the breath can change your experience of the moment.

NOTES

1. Sarah Mattice, personal communication, July 14, 2020.
2. Note that some conflict can be productive; deliberation and dialogue may produce conflicting viewpoints and still remain productive. Unproductivity arises when participants stop listening in favor of entrenching their own positions.

Chapter 2

Who and How Will We Be?
Creating Constructive Conversations

Conversation begins with curiosity, with inquiry, with listening. We know that conversation demands active listening, but so often we listen in order to formulate response and counterargument, rather than listen to hear and understand. We converse to speak rather than to hear. We inquire to negate rather than to consider. Yet deep and active listening is essential for truly constructive conversations to occur, as it is imperative that each party be recognized and understood. This understanding doesn't necessarily entail agreement, but it does demand awareness. As Valarie Kaur has written, "Deep listening is an act of surrender" (Kaur 2020, 143), wherein we work to release our preconceptions, our biases, and even our need to win an argument. It makes us vulnerable and thus requires our courage. It takes mindful effort and practice and, even with these, deep listening can be derailed by our emotional triggers. Hence the ongoing practice. Yet the practice is invaluable for constructive conversations and transformed communities: "The more I listen, the less I hate. The less I hate, the more I am free to choose actions that are controlled not by animosity but by wisdom" (Kaur 2020, 140).

We can train ourselves in deep listening, in empathy (the focus of chapter 3), and in pedagogical practices that foster dialogue over debate, consensus over conquest, and perspective over myopia. One system for developing these skills is deliberative pedagogy.

Chapter 2

THE ROLE OF DELIBERATIVE PEDAGOGY

Historically,

> A liberal arts education is intended to cultivate a capacity for reasoned deliberation, critical thinking, and good judgment. While these goals for student development have long been associated with Americans' understanding of an appropriate college education (Hartley), the task of achieving such outcomes has become increasingly difficult over the past several decades. Professors at U.S. institutions are now tasked not simply with honing these skills, but often with introducing them to students. (Strachan 2017, n.p.)

Couple this with the fact that the humanities and liberal arts education are increasingly perceived as less valuable than STEM-focused educational paths, and we can see how student preparedness in these capacities has not been emphasized to the degree it had been historically. As a result, we are seeing a different society than that of the past, one in which too few citizens understand their responsibilities as citizens and have developed the skills necessary for managing conflict and reaching consensus. Mainstream U.S. culture has focused on individual rights to the detriment of collective responsibility, and those who have historically attended to collective responsibility have been the marginalized and oppressed. Deliberative pedagogy attempts to bring back to the classroom the skills of listening and reasoned dialogue, along with a sense of civic responsibility.

According to Timothy J. Shaffer, "Deliberative pedagogy is a democratic educational process and a way of thinking that encourages students to encounter and consider multiple perspectives, weigh trade-offs and tensions, and move toward action through informed judgment" (Shaffer 2017, n.p.). It allows students practice in decision making, informed judgment, and civil discourse toward engagement with critical issues in the classroom and in the communities beyond it. For example, a classroom modeled on deliberative pedagogy might allow students to help determine key elements of the syllabus, based on a framework first provided by the professor. Such a classroom will likely engage students in decisions regarding discussion guidelines and assignments in keeping with the professor's course objectives. It might also ask students to put forward their own learning objectives and deliberate on ways these objectives, along with those the professor deems necessary, might be realized.

In "Deliberative Pedagogy as a Central Tenet: First-Year Students Develop a Course and a Community," Leila R. Brammer relates the experience of teaching a first-year course with deliberative pedagogy as the central content and engaged practice. In the course, "Deliberation, Democracy, and Civility," students were instrumental in determining the final syllabus (adapted from a working template that Brammer had provided), assignments, processes, and schedule. According to student reflections at the end of the course, they noted the freedom and empowerment that came when they were made cocreators of their own learning experience. Brammer also summarizes that students "discussed how they gained a sense of their place in the community and noted that everyone respected each individual's autonomy and his or her role in the class. They spoke of the class as a model for how to live together" (Brammer 2017, n.p.). Thus, deliberative pedagogy provides practical knowledge that results in skills for living in community.

Beyond such a classroom, students might find themselves organizing public forums on the central course topics, bringing their classroom learning to bear on community issues, and engaging the community in dialogue toward action. According to Strachan, "Deliberation includes discursive efforts to identify solutions for shared, public problems in a process characterized by open, inclusive exchanges. Further, the participants in this process should engage in reason giving, consider one another's perspectives, and treat each other as equals" (Strachan 2017, n.p.). Many educators may already be working with processes of deliberative pedagogy, helping students work through relevant issues with reason-based conversation, openness to multiple perspectives, and informed judgment that strives for consensus—even though consensus might not be achieved. In fact, as Al-Atiyat has argued, consensus may not be the point: "My goal is to teach students a process of making decisions by considering multiple options, listening to each other, and acknowledging biases and points of privilege" (Al-Atiyat 2017, n.p.), all of which will help them engage in civil discourse in the public realm, a practice that seemingly has fallen by the way-side. Yet these practices "help move political participation beyond an adversarial (and likely ill-informed) process that pits citizens against one another and toward an exchange characterized by inclusiveness, mutual respect, and reason giving" (Strachan 2017, n.p.).

Deliberative pedagogy is a useful model for classes that engage the topics of race, justice, and social responsibility. Since these are topics that often arouse diverse perspectives, a framework of deliberative pedagogy lays the foundation for these perspectives to be heard while consensus on the best course for social action is sought. Students then come to understand their own and others' perspectives more fully while honing the skills of deliberation, discernment, and consensus building. The practices of rhetoric and argumentation are utilized and these skills are augmented; students practice reasoned argument, learning to support their claims, seek common ground, refute faulty oppositional arguments, and concede to those that are well reasoned. These steps of asserting, judging, accepting, or rejecting are publicly performed, allowing participants to witness the process and allowing a meta-level understanding of the process to be delineated by the facilitator.

Students are given the opportunity to analyze the issue as well as understand the process of deliberation about the issue. In the former case, students begin to understand the contours of a public issue—to give and receive reasons for a certain course of action, to judge the pros and cons of various options and opportunities. In the latter case, students are made more fully aware of the norms and values that allow such a deliberative process to take place—respect for multiple viewpoints and opportunities for those viewpoints to be voiced, heard, and understood before they are judged and acted upon.

Classes that emphasize deliberative pedagogy offer the opportunity for transformation as students broaden their knowledge, refine their argumentation skills, practice public deliberation, and gain a level of understanding of how consensus is achieved. This transformation is both individual and collective within the classroom and potentially within the community, provided students engage their skills and fulfill their action plans beyond the classroom. For the race- and justice-focused classroom, "transformation means students from different backgrounds and races coming together as part of their education to have deliberative conversations about the possibilities for a more just and equitable society—and their roles in creating this society as citizens and future professionals" (Shaffer 2017, n.p.).

Educators hoping to utilize a framework of deliberative pedagogy should be up-front about the nature of the classroom, alerting students to the fact that the class is as much about the skills necessary for public deliberation as about the content of the course. Offer an overview of the processes of deliberation and civil discourse. Emphasize that the classroom is a community and that consensus is desirable, even if not always achievable. Reinforce the importance of listening rather than having the last word, and help students be aware of who typically has access to these conversations. Additionally, teach students the etiquette of entering and engaging in such conversations, laying ground rules that are perhaps developed in collaboration with students. These might include the importance of

- asking questions rather than always asserting opinions,
- using inclusive language,
- defining terms that are unfamiliar and that will become part of the class's lexicon,
- speaking for oneself, and
- respecting everyone's privacy.

Educators are meant to be facilitators of this dialogic experience and the mutual learning that takes place via these conversations. They are creating the space that allows and respects polyvocality and the resultant learning that will occur from it. The role of the facilitator is that of space-maker: "Creating and holding space for authentic and productive dialogue, conversations that can ultimately be not only educational but also transformative" (Shaffer 2017, n.p.). In this context, educators are not just teaching content but are teaching skills. Deliberative pedagogy provides a framework for the development of skills in critical thinking, reasoned argument, open-mindedness, empathy, and sound judgment. For these reasons, deliberative pedagogy is also a logical framework for mindful conversations about race and social justice.

THE CLASSROOM: MINDFUL DELIBERATIVE PEDAGOGY

What people think about race is often foundational, a primary basis on which they form their identities and evaluate others, even though these thought processes are often unconscious (and hence why I try to make students aware of them early in a course through the "Who Am I?" personal statement). Participating in dialogue that challenges foundational beliefs is emotional—not just intellectual—work. Thus, those of us who facilitate these dialogues need to remember that emotional responses are inevitable, typically not explored, and can take a multitude of forms—anger, guilt, shame, denial, hope, empathy, and so on—within the same conversation and even within the same person. A white person hearing about white supremacy and white privilege for the first time might respond with disbelief, denial, and anger, in keeping with what Robin DiAngelo describes in *White Fragility*. A person of color might then respond with anger, a sense of being invalidated, and a desire to educate—or a sense of exhaustion at having to educate yet again. These emotions are real, and our deliberate response to them can mean the difference between a constructive conversation and one that spirals into vilification and divisiveness.

A clear goal of most race-critical classrooms is social justice, which, in the framework of deliberative pedagogy, might be recognized as "a connection between education and democracy" (Shaffer 2017, n.p.). I am not suggesting that democracy and social justice are the same thing or that the latter necessarily results from the former; throughout the history of the United States, we have clearly seen that it does not. But deliberative pedagogy consciously develops in students the skills of productive citizenship, a skill set that seekers of social justice actively employ.[1]

In the forward to *Deliberative Pedagogy: Teaching and Learning for Democratic Engagement*, David Mathews writes "Being a good citizen . . . is commendable. But it isn't enough. It isn't enough because there are difficult problems that can't be solved without collective action by citizens. It isn't enough because people can't act together when they disagree about how to act.

It isn't enough because, without joining forces, citizens don't have the power to make a difference in their communities and beyond" (Mathews 2017, n.p.). The anti-racist classroom is usually intended to be a place of deliberative pedagogy, though too often educators hope to build a social justice bridge in the classroom without recognizing that not everyone is beginning with the same tools. Furthermore, individuals' abilities to build this bridge may be impeded by their varied states of being—including their emotional realities. One person may feel fueled and empowered to begin the project while another might be dismayed at the amount of work still to be done. Alternatively, there may be people who don't see the need for a bridge at all.

Thus, deliberative pedagogy must be coupled with mindfulness, with intentional attention to individuals' emotional and physical realities and the ways in which these realities shape thoughts, perceptions, and experiences of self and others. A preliminary consideration for encouraging emotional and physical well-being is the classroom space itself.

ATTENTION TO THE CLASSROOM SPACE

The classroom—even when it is online—is a space we visit with our intellects, our bodies, and our emotions. Because of this, attention should be paid to what we want this space to include. Before delving into deep conversation, the establishment of ground rules and expectations is a common consideration. And to cultivate a sense of shared investment in and commitment to the work of the classroom, students should be involved in the establishment of guiding principles for conversation and community building in the classroom. Of course, the educator may come to the door with set expectations, but these should be relayed to the class for their feedback, amendments, and additional requests. For example, the introduction to a diversity workshop held at my university stated:

> We acknowledge that you all come to this space with different lived experiences, points of view, and levels of knowledge and comfort with this subject matter. These expectations are meant to intentionally create a space where we can each contribute and bring our whole selves. This is a place where we can learn and grow with each other, where no one is disposable. Trust in your capacity to make discoveries and work through/lean into disagreement and discomfort. If a concept comes up for you that you don't like or rubs you the wrong way, think about why it bothers you. Hold onto what works for you! ("Train the Trainer" 2017)

Initial expectations at this workshop included respectfully getting uncomfortable (sharing by choice), checking presumptions at the door, not competing for airtime, and using I-statements.

These expectations are only a few of what might be established in collaboration among educators and students, facilitators, and participants. Others might include guidelines such as *get out of your comfort zone and out of the combat zone*; *talk "with" rather than "at"*; *remember that learning is a process, not an end-point*; *pay attention to your body language, striving for openness*. These expectations and guidelines can help us stay mindful of our emotions, our posture and body language, the spirit we bring to the work of dialogue and discovery, and the way all of these factors influence our communications with others.

In addition to remaining mindful of our energy and attitude during dialogue, we can pay attention to the physical classroom space. What is the lighting like? Are the chairs comfortable? Can seating be set in a circle to cultivate a more democratic environment? Even the close proximity of drinking water and restrooms can go a long way toward adding comfort in what are often uncomfortable conversations, as can natural lighting and a view of nature. For those with more control over physical space, the ability to play soft music for those entering a room can aid in setting a relaxed and welcoming atmosphere. This can be accomplished online too, as the virtual classroom allows us to play music before we begin. All of these physical factors can forward the process of creating "Gracious Space," which moves beyond the physical into the realm of the emotional or the "spirit" of the work we undertake. The Center for Ethical Leadership discusses Gracious Space[2] as a set of principles that can "build team, trust and communities. It can be introduced as a core part of the culture and to create learning organizations. It can serve as a guide to change agents and facilitators in their change work." The center defines Gracious Space as a "<u>spirit</u> and a <u>setting</u> where we <u>invite the stranger</u> and <u>learn in public</u>" ("Creating Gracious Space" 2021, emphasis mine), and they identify a number of practical steps that can be taken to build such space:

Pay Attention to Spirit: compassion, curiosity, "being" Gracious Space
Create Intentional Spaces
Invite the "Stranger": when diverse perspective is beneficial
Learn in Public: open your heart and mind to the thinking of others
Build Trust: through character, competence, consistency and information
Inquire: seek first to understand
Listen Deeply and Slow Down ("Creating Gracious Space" 2021)

INVITING AND WELCOMING

Although educators begin a class with learning objectives already printed in the syllabus, we should make room for students' goals for learning as well. What are our ideals and values as a class? What are we seeking to learn and what skills do we wish to build in this space? And how can we manifest these ideals and values, first here in the classroom and then in the broader communities we enter when we leave this space? Additionally, who are the students we're teaching? When we're focusing on issues of race in the classroom, educators too often center the white students in the class—often forgetting the different standpoints, experiences, and educational needs of students of color, a reality that will be explored in more detail later.

Important questions to answer are *Who are we inviting? Who is being welcomed?* All participants should be welcomed, and everyone's needs should be attended to. As mentioned previously, conversations should be accessible for everyone present and everyone should have the agency to speak. This agency is facilitated through clear guidelines on how participants should move into and out of the conversation. Additionally, the facilitator can offer subtle cues that encourage over-talkers to make room for others and that call on the typically silent to offer their opinions. Best practices for accessibility in online classes suggest helping students find comfort with speaking and listening in synchronous classes (or sharing and responding in asynchronous classes). Practical ways of doing this include participation expectations that are clearly spelled out at the beginning of a course. In many of my asynchronous online classes, I specify how many responses to classmates students are expected to offer, and I am clear about what constitutes a deep and engaged response. In synchronous classes, a greater sense of community can be created when participants join the class with their video on, allowing us a greater awareness of their facial expressions, as we would have in a face-to-face class. Of course, teachers of online classes must also be mindful of the fatigue that can develop when people are on screen and feel overly an object of attention.

Participants can be encouraged to speak with compassionate honesty about their own realities and listen to others' realities with compassionate belief, refraining from demonizing others or meeting others' experiences with doubt or critique. Mindful attention to others, which includes clear seeing and intent listening, is part of *Metta*, the Buddhist practice of loving-kindness addressed in this chapter's mindfulness and movement practices. This attention is intentional and is an opportunity for transforming a classroom into an inclusive community where difference is respected rather than devalued. Practicing this level of civility in a classroom space is also an opportunity for developing the skills necessary to bring civility into the public realm and to confront difference—and even social injustice—without creating more division and rancor. In speaking to Freedom Riders in 1960, Martin Luther King, Jr. said, "Our ultimate end must be the creation of the beloved community." The microcosm of the classroom can be a space for skills building toward that beloved community.

RESPONDING TO RESISTANCE

The classroom, as a microcosm of larger society, is a place where we can hone the skills and practice the virtues we hope to enact in civic settings. It is a place where most of us haven't been trained to remain mindful of ourselves beyond our intellectual capacities and growth. A mind-body-spirit connection isn't what most of us are accustomed to thinking about in an academic setting, yet if we hope to offer mindful attention to our classroom conversations, we must take conscious steps toward recognizing that we don't exist in classrooms as disembodied intellectuals and we must recognize the price paid for too little attention to our students' (and our own) fully emotional, physical, and intellectual selves. We have paid this price through conversations filled with animosity and debate rather than empathy and dialogue, conversations that have been divisive rather than constructive. In addition, too often we have overlooked or not understood how to respond to resistance, in ourselves and in the students we are guiding in the learning process.

Resistance can be seen and felt in multiple ways. Even as facilitators, we might feel anger or fear that we then follow mindlessly. In students, we might see rolling eyes and crossed arms, a refusal to look others in the face. We might encounter adamant disagreement and outright denial in students who refuse to consider another perspective. What are our options as educators and facilitators in these situations? These, too, are multiple, but if we are trying to create constructive conversations and encourage positive social change, then we must practice mindfulness in our responses: take a breath, listen closely, and respond to the basic issue in question. We can train ourselves to recognize and assess our own emotions and then re-route our responses in more productive ways. We can also ask students to take this mindful pause to breathe, actively hear, and understand; we can ask students to restate what they hear another person saying, allowing the first speaker to be fully heard and to correct any misunderstandings. This also allows the listener clarity on what has been said before they offer a response.

Mindfulness meditation is an exceptionally strong method for preparing one in the skill of recognition and choice when dealing with our emotional responses and their ability to influence thoughts. In the face of student resistance, fact-based responses often are the best option, although "flipping the script" scenarios (finding a way to put a student in someone else's shoes) can also be effective as they can encourage empathy and help us point out the logical fallacies on which resistance and disagreement so often unsteadily rest. A number of other steps we can take include attention to patterns of thought and language use:

Encourage both/and thinking. One of the benefits of postmodern theories is that they have trained us to recognize that seemingly conflicting ideas can be held in tandem—that we can survive cognitive dissonance. We need not bind our thinking or our systems to the either/or logical fallacy. In discussing anti-racism, bell hooks declares, "Anti-racist work requires of all of us vigilance about the ways we use language. Either/or thinking is crucial to the maintenance of racism and other forms of group oppression. Whenever we think in terms of both/and we are better situated to do the work of community building" (hooks 2003, 37).

Along these lines, we must also *attend to language use* in general—ours and our students'. Defining relevant vocabulary and setting up expectations for inclusive language at the beginning can help overcome resistance in students. There are times when students resist joining a conversation simply because they are unfamiliar with the jargon or worried about using terms that may be offensive. Honest, nonjudgmental dialogue about what terms students have heard, where they derive from, and why some are considered offensive offers a basic level of understanding that is necessary for participants to have some common ground. Set the stage, reminding students that in making a list of relevant (and offensive) terms, we are working toward a common language for conversation—what we mean and what we don't mean; what we will condone and what we will deem inexcusable. Then ask them to list words they have heard in conversations about race, adding others you think will prove useful. Define those that students don't seem to understand, and discuss the histories that explain why certain terms are considered offensive. Develop a shared vocabulary so that students can converse with a baseline of understanding.

When tensions and conflict seem particularly high and unsurpassable, I've sometimes found it best to *move outside*, often figuratively and sometimes literally. In the *Witness: Agent* exercise, participants can be guided in moving outside of their emotional responses in order to see them more clearly. At other times, participants can be asked to change their location and engage in a shared exercise that may help them arrive at a new understanding; this is the *Walking Talk* exercise. See the mindfulness and movement practices at the end of this chapter for instructions on these two practices.

Pre-emptive steps can also help educators curb resistance that might be expected in certain conversations. For those in university settings, a content statement in the syllabus about the nature of the course can be helpful in making students aware of the conversations to come. (Of course, this can also result in disinterested or antagonistic students self-selecting out of a course.) As Brené Brown has noted, when we ask people to be vulnerable, we are asking them to be open to wounding. As educators, we must remain aware of the wounding potential of these difficult conversations, of the difficult emotions they often generate, and of the difficult knowledge they are capable of creating.[3] We can prepare students by being explicit about the fact that these conversations will be challenging and uncomfortable and that we as facilitators are present to help keep them safe. We can also encourage them with the reminder that learning—in other words growth and positive change—is the ultimate goal.

In nearly every class I teach, I stress the fact that I am not there to dictate anyone's belief, change anyone's thinking, or mandate anyone's feelings. As an educator, I think my role in every class is to encourage students to understand their own belief systems and from where they arise, to decide their own thinking on specific topics and the validity of their conclusions, and to be honest about their own feelings and then conscious of how they will respond in relationship to others. My role is to get students asking the questions *Who am I? How should I be? And how can I best exist in relationship with others?* Simply put, *who am I when I am being my best self, and how can I be that self more often?* These are mindfulness questions that, when individually answered, can lead to much more productive conversations and relationships. I encourage students to ask these questions of themselves, even if they never share their answers with me. bell hooks has written, "As educators, one of the best things that we can do for our students is to not force them into holding theories and solid concepts but rather to encourage the process, the inquiry involved, and the times of not knowing—with all of the uncertainties that go along with that. This is really what supports going deep. This is openness" (hooks 2003, 48).

Finally, *always allow time for reflection and processing to conclude a conversation.* This can involve a "temperature check" wherein each person is asked to give a one- or two-word sense of where he or she is as the conversation concludes. These usually take the form of adjectives: hopeful, angry, uneasy, enlightened, and so on. An alternative is to have students undertake the "Known/New" exercise. Students are asked to write down what they knew (or thought they knew) before the conversation as well as something new they learned. This new knowledge may negate what the student thought they knew, might reenforce it, or might be unrelated to it. The point is that students are able to clarify, deepen, add to their knowledge, and move toward open understanding.

CREATING AN ANTI-RACIST CLASSROOM

Openness is crucial to engaging in constructive conversations. Yet even as educators, our assumptions, expectations, language, interventions/noninterventions, assignments, and grading practices contribute to the racialized nature of our classrooms. Even classrooms can reinforce racism, destroying the openness, inclusivity, and anti-racist goals we strive to reach. "To build community requires vigilant awareness of the work we must continually do to undermine all the socialization that leads us to behave in ways that perpetuate domination" (hooks 2003, 36). Here, hooks is pointing to the fact that we must be continually mindful of the sources of our beliefs and attitudes in order to make conscious choices in our responses. Ibram Kendi writes pointedly about racist educational spaces in *How to Be an Antiracist* when he discusses his third-grade experiences with a white teacher who didn't see or call on students of color. Scholarship on this reality traces it from elementary schools through university settings, and students of color know it exhaustingly well, leading Deanna M. Blackwell to ask the crucial question: "What counts as anti-racist education for students of color?" (Blackwell 2010, 473). Acknowledging that many educators have tried to bring anti-racist consciousness into classroom settings, Blackwell notes, "critical educators have oriented their practice towards bringing white students into a consciousness about white privilege and racism . . . or towards examining the effect that racial-identity politics have on classroom interactions" (Blackwell 2010, 473). In effect, "anti-racist education, even in its attempt to uncover the subtleties of racism, continues to be preoccupied with white students at the expense of students of color" (Blackwell 2010, 474).

For a classroom to be anti-racist in its practices as well as its content, it must recognize the needs and objectives of students of color too. The classroom needs to empower these students in their own learning goals and personal development, rather than leaving them to function as "cultural experts, [teacher's] aides and witnesses" (Blackwell 2010, 485). Commonly, students of color who find themselves in one of these three roles will speak up or remain silent. If they speak, they risk being "perceived as volunteering to be a resource and an ally" on the white students' journey toward racial consciousness (Blackwell 2010, 484). If they remain silent, they become witnesses to the white students' expanding awareness, limiting students of color who want conversations about race to move beyond a burgeoning racial epiphany. Blackwell attests:

> My education in the anti-racist classroom has functioned more like participant observation in the field of whiteness. What I have learned in these classes has been overwhelmingly how white students experience the process of race consciousness-raising. I have wondered if there is a classroom space in which we, students of color, can be transformed and guided in our intellectual endeavors as opposed to being unofficially trained as experts on whiteness. (Blackwell 2010, 487)

In the typical race-critical classroom, the educational needs of students of color are marginalized in favor white students' education, belying the intention to be anti-racist.

What would make classrooms anti-racist in practice as well as theory? While not an exhaustive list, the following criteria serve as a starting point for creating spaces where students of color are not marginalized in favor of white students' racial awakening.

- Educators must be aware of the emotional labor students of color are often expected to undertake in guiding white students to realizations about race, racism, and identity.
- Educators should actively combat this positioning of students of color by noticing it when it happens; redirecting conversation (to emphasize facts and texts); and allowing room for critical examination of race, racism, and identity for *all* students in the class, regardless of their level of race consciousness.
- Blackwell observes that when a classroom is "organized by the educational needs of white students, a silent decision is made that the 'whole class' is not yet primed for advanced academic explorations into race" (Blackwell 2010, 487). Yet educators should equally prioritize space for students of color to do their own growing and identity development in classrooms, encouraging them (as any other student) to establish their own goals and abilities within each class. Educators can work with white students to develop anti-racism skills, while also actively fostering a classroom environment where students of color are equally empowered toward their own individual growth and personal development.
- Consider establishing separate, safe spaces for students of color and white students within/before certain conversations. White students may need additional time and guidance to realize the racial realities of students of color, without students of color being relied upon to do the emotional labor of educating them. And students of color often benefit from spaces where they can pursue their own lines of educational and personal development. Not only can separate "caucuses" benefit students' academic goals, they can also serve as places for interrogating the varied experiences students of color have in negotiating academic conversations on race; they have the opportunity for meta-level awareness of these conversations and, consequently, their own emotional and intellectual responses to them. Such a space models a true decentering of whiteness (Blackwell 2010, 492) from which students of color can protect their academic selves (Blackwell 2010, 490), thus advancing their own knowledge and educational goals.
- Educators should remain cognizant of intersectional realities, recognizing that all people experience contexts wherein portions of their identity are more salient and that these intersectionalities are experienced at often un-seen levels. In other words, none of us can assume what another is experiencing in any given moment. Knowing this, we should leave space for individuals to

express (or not) the full complexities of their emotional and physical realities as they choose, and we should refrain from making assumptions about others.
- Educators should respond to auto-ethnographic work with deep thought and care *before* the work is made available for a whole-class response, if it is made available at all. This is especially important in online classes, where discussion boards are often used. Educators should make sure that students are witnessing the processes of compassion-based critical analysis before requiring students to perform such analyses themselves.

THE ONLINE CLASSROOM

The online classroom can be imagined as a space similar to a physical classroom, wherein students need to feel invited and welcomed, seen and heard. This is easier to achieve when classes are taught synchronously and through video, because we have the real-time experience of seeing each other, reading visual cues, and so forth. Special attention should be given to asynchronous classes where discussion is text-based. It is helpful to post "Netiquette" rules—guidelines for internet etiquette—so that students know the expectations haven't changed from a face-to-face classroom. They are still tasked with remaining diplomatic, with recognizing the human beings with whom they are interacting. And, of course, the facilitator is a model for the kind of interaction that is expected of participants. Modeling gracious behavior shows participants methods for responding to and mediating conflict, for listening with attention, and for dialoguing with compassion.

HOW TO HAVE DIFFICULT CONVERSATIONS

In the early weeks of one semester, I asked the students in Black American Literature to brainstorm with me about how we should have the sometimes difficult, often uncomfortable conversations we would have about race, identity, and justice. This conversation led us into thoughts about not only how to have the conversations but how to *be*—how did we want to exist as people in relationship to and in community with other people? What behaviors did we want to demonstrate? What attitudes and habits did we want to cultivate? Here is what we decided:

Slow Down

Slowing down is a first step. Difficult conversations are involved and laborious. They take time, so we need to give ourselves and others the necessary time to feel, to process, to think, and to respond. Facilitators can aid in this process by allowing room for silence. When a question arises, facilitators often rush to fill the uncomfortable silence with their own perspectives or with additional questions. Or participants can rush in before they have taken time to parse their thoughts and feelings. Allowing adequate time for each question and for the conversation as a whole is essential, even if it means abandoning a preconceived schedule to follow the direction and depth that seem possible in a given moment. Facilitators can mention at the outset their intention to allow silence as an intentional creative space and to allow discomfort as a site of growth.

Allow Discomfort

Growth entails discomfort, and we need to be willing to be uncomfortable if we hope to learn and expand in awareness, knowledge, and connection. As we are pushing through the crust of past perceptions, we feel the scratch and the constraint, but pushing past moves us into a more expansive space where new growth can unfurl.

Listen Actively

Active listening entails attending to another's words and body language, giving respectful attention to what they are saying in order that we understand them. Conversations that engage active listening are ones in which people feel heard, seen, and respected. Such conditions help foster mutual understanding and consensus, rather than divisiveness and debate, and they build healthier communities. Habitually, we often listen in order to respond or argue, but what if we actively work to hear and understand another's point of view?

When we listen mindfully, we pay attention to the words being spoken and the embodied signals of the speaker. We work to hear the words without judgment and critique, without formulating a response or fixating on a narrative we construct in our own heads about what the person is saying or what it means for us. And we pay attention to our own emotional responses to their words before we react or respond. Obviously, conversation is two-way, so responses are necessary, but when we listen actively, we allow space for and attention to another's truth before we formulate a response. We recognize our own emotional reactions and then consciously decide on the best response. One exercise to practice is the classic "restatement" technique: after you hear someone speak, try to paraphrase what they have said. We may use phrases such as "What I hear you saying is" or "It sounds like you're saying." We can then attend to the emotional resonances of that person's words, working to understand what that reality is like for them. Once a person's reality is validated in this way, he or she feels acknowledged and much more relaxed. He or she is also more inclined to listen to you with the same respect.

Mindful listening exercises throughout daily life also can train us in this type of active listening, making it more possible for us to listen actively in conversation with others. For example, try listening to all of the sounds around you right now, without analyzing or judging them. Try to identify what each is and then move on to the next sound, not holding on to thoughts about the sounds but simply listening to them.

Be Polite

This is such a basic guideline, but one that we can forget in the heat of emotions or in the remoteness of social media.

> Polite interactions involve soliciting others' opinions, qualifying one's claims, providing supportive feedback, acknowledging others' contributions, and avoiding confrontation. All of these conversational patterns encourage collaboration and are especially useful when assessing future undertakings. In contrast, interactions characterized by challenges, disagreements, and interruptions lead to entrenched positions, especially when these tactics are used in public. (Strachan 2017, n.p.)

In the public realm, we can think of politeness as diplomacy, which involves efforts toward understanding and common ground, positive rather than negative language use, and the avoidance of accusations. Even when we disagree, we can be diplomatic.

Instead of "I disagree," we might say:
    I see what you mean, but . . .
    I agree with your point. However, I also think . . .
    I think a more productive avenue might be . . .
Instead of "You're not making sense" or "You're not being clear":
    I don't understand.
    Can you help me understand what you mean by . . .
Instead of "You don't understand me":
    I don't think I'm being clear.

Politeness and diplomacy signal respect and cultivate it in return.

Take Turns

In William Golding's novel *Lord of the Flies*, the boys hold a conch shell as a symbol of who holds the floor. As their attempts to remain civilized erode, the conch is forgotten, pointing to the fact that their ability to listen and enact patience is essential to their civil discourse. So, too, is ours. Training ourselves in active listening is an exercise in patience, openness, and awareness. It's a true mindfulness exercise, as it demands that we wait and even work through our discomfort before we can proceed with reasoned thought and consciously chosen language.

Don't interrupt

See all of the aforementioned points.

Speak "with" not "to"

This, too, is part of active listening. When we are able to speak with someone, we are engaging in mutually respectful dialogue, rather than demagoguery or lecture. And we invite them to do the same with us. A different atmosphere is created by sitting down in a circle to speak with people rather than speaking to them from a pulpit. Keep in mind that a primary goal should be for you to understand what the other is trying to convey, without the weight of your predeterminations and preconditioned judgments. Cultivating this atmosphere of nonjudgmental understanding is challenging, but it is the same nonjudgmental awareness that we cultivate through mindfulness exercises. The more we practice the skill of mindfulness in daily life, the more easily it will come into play in our interactions with others.

Remember You're Talking with **Someone**

Most of us have seen the rabid attacks that can take place on social media or the ways in which social media "trolls" dehumanize others (not to mention the way we dehumanize by using such a term). Keep in mind that you're speaking with a person who, like you, feels emotions and believes in a set of values that are as important to them as yours are to you. Cultivating common ground is easier when we begin from a position that recognizes another's humanity. Valarie Kaur writes about this through the concept of *wonder*: "If we are safe and nurtured enough to develop our capacity to wonder, we start to wonder about the people in our lives, too—their thoughts and experiences, their pain and joy, their wants and needs. We begin to sense that they are to themselves as vast and complex as we are to ourselves, their inner world as infinite as our own. In other words, we are seeing them as our equal" (Kaur 2020, 10).

Feeling safe within ourselves is an important starting point, one that demands we attend to our emotional responses to others' words. This sense of safety is enhanced when we recognize we needn't take another's disagreement with us as *personal*; their differing opinion does not negate our own. Their disagreement does not diminish us, does not reflect on our intelligence.

And we don't need to convince them of our rightness in order to remain on solid ground ourselves. We might try looking at disagreement as a curiosity rather than a threat: *How interesting that our individual lives have led us to such different conclusions.* This thought—as opposed to *I must defend my side and win!*—can lead us to questions that foster understanding. *What has led you to your conclusion? What in your experience has helped you see things this way?* And these deepening questions are more likely to lead us to mutual respect, if not common ground.

Be Compassionate and Empathetic

I also find it helpful to see emotions through the lens of only two: love and fear. Other emotions are rooted in one or the other of these. When I trace the emotion I'm feeling to its root, I can assess whether my emotion is helpful or harmful. If it's love-based, it's helpful. If it's fear-based, it's usually not, unless I need to flee from danger. Many times we feel the need to fight or flee from perceived danger even in conversation: *They don't agree with me. They're demanding that I fight for my beliefs or relinquish them. I need to defend myself and win in order to survive.* But these perceived dangers might be imagined in other ways: *they're asking me to reimagine something I believe. I feel strongly rooted in my belief and can therefore listen and speak without defensiveness. Their disagreement doesn't make my belief wrong. I don't need to take this situation personally.*

I also need to remember that others' emotions are based in either love or fear. When I can recognize that someone's anger is really an expression of their often unconscious fears, I can respond with more compassion and less defensiveness. As Valarie Kaur has wisely written, "Empathy is cognitive *and* emotional—to inhabit another person's view of the world is to *feel* the world with them. But I also know that it's okay if I don't feel very much for them at all. I just need to feel safe enough to stay curious" (Kaur 2020, 143).

Be Courageous

This courage takes many forms. Sometimes it's more courageous to be silent than to speak. To listen to uncomfortable truths rather than speak against them. Sometimes, courage is in speaking up for ourselves or for others whose voices have been marginalized. Sometimes it's found in taking up the role of ally. Sometimes in teaching. Always in continuing to learn and refusing to be boxed in, even by our own perspectives. For example, when you find yourself immediately disagreeing with someone, try to stretch your imagination, engage in empathy, and ask the vital question, *What if what this person is saying is actually true?* "We [may] have drawn close to the story and lost ourselves in another's experience, but we haven't [always] returned to ourselves and asked: What does this demand of *me*?" (Kaur 2020, 144). Yet we need to ask this question. If what this person is saying is actually true, consider what that would mean for you, your perspectives on life, your understanding of the world. Then see where this might take you in conversation—and community—with that person with whom you want to disagree.

Question rather than Assume or Accuse

This task involves staying open to wonder, which means we acknowledge and stay curious about what we don't know. Charles Johnson writes: "I prefer to see the Other as a great and glorious mystery about whom I can never make any ironclad assumptions or judgments" (Johnson 2014, 28). Attending to this mystery means we take the time and make the effort to know another's perspective, to respect another's reality. Asking questions, rather than issuing judgments and vilifying others' thoughts and feelings will point us in a more productive conversational direction, allowing the opportunity for common ground to be found.

Prioritize the Process

Finally, remember that the process is often as important, if not more so, than the content of a conversation. As Derald Wing Sue notes, "Race talk is often not about the substance of an argument, but a cover for what is actually happening" with participants' unidentified and troubling emotions. Thus, facilitators "need understand not only the content of the communication but also the process resulting from the interpersonal dynamics" (Sue 2015, 228). In *Race Talk and the Conspiracy of Silence*, Sue details some of the common emotional responses individuals might experience when engaging in racial dialogues and some of the common statements that issue from these emotions. For example, someone might say, "I could be doing more" which might be read as *I feel guilty* or "I'm not responsible for any of this," which often means *I feel defensive* (Sue 2015, 237). Understanding this verbal shorthand for common yet complex emotions can help facilitators identify and get to the root of participants' responses, promoting more productive conversation and potentially meaningful insights. Sue also highlights five ineffective responses facilitators often give and then delineates eleven effective strategies for encouraging constructive conversation:

Ineffective Strategies
 1. Doing nothing
 2. Sidetracking the conversation
 3. Appeasing the participants

4. Terminating the discussion
5. Becoming defensive

Effective Strategies
1. Understanding one's racial/cultural identity
2. Acknowledging and being open to admitting one's racial biases
3. Being comfortable and open to discussing topics of race and racism
4. Understanding the meaning of emotions
5. Validating and facilitating discussion of feelings
6. Controlling the process and not the content of race talk
7. Unmasking the difficult dialogue through process observations and interventions
8. Not allowing a difficult dialogue to be brewed in silence
9. Understanding differences in communication styles
10. Forewarning, planning, and purposefully instigating race talk
11. Validating, encouraging, and expressing admiration and appreciation to participants who speak when it is unsafe[4] to do so (Sue 2015, 230–244)

Thus, Sue reminds us that facilitators have ample work to do in preparing themselves—both emotionally and cognitively—for effectively leading dialogues on race. We cannot effectively engage in constructive conversations about difficult topics without this preparation and without helping to prepare those with whom we will converse. Remaining mindful of our own state of being—and helping participants become more mindful of their own—is preliminary work for these demanding conversations. The mindfulness and movement practices offered in the following section are particularly helpful in this regard, allowing us self-reflection and insight when we are preparing for a challenging conversation and even when we find ourselves already in the midst of one.

NOTES

1. I am also not trying to romanticize social justice activists or suggest that they have perfected the skills of citizenship, or that they always use the most effective means to reach their desired ends.

2. I am indebted to my colleague Chris Janson for first bringing to my attention the Center for Ethical Leadership and its concept of Gracious Space.

3. And as Bettina L. Love has reminded us, as educators we must also be aware of the toll this work takes on us and actively cultivate the spaces necessary for our own support, strength, and resiliency.

4. Again, I would differentiate unsafe moments (which should be alleviated by the facilitator) from uncomfortable ones (which are right and necessary).

Mindfulness and Movement Practices

*BODY

*Note: Always use extreme caution when beginning or facilitating a new movement practice. Practitioners may be advised to consult a medical professional or trained movement specialist before attempting specific body-based practices. Facilitators should remind practitioners that they must not move in any way that will be injurious or cause pain.

Mountain Pose

This is a beneficial pose to use when the class has been sitting in conversation for a time, as it realigns posture, creating more room for energizing breath. It's also helpful if people are feeling isolated, insignificant, or anxious—imagining ourselves as mountains in a mountain range provides us with an image of strength, stability, and continuity with others.

To Practice

1. Ask students to stand next to their desks. Have them plant their feet hip-distance apart, which anatomically is only about two fists-width of space. The outer edges of the feet should be parallel, and students should be instructed to feel all four corners of their feet firmly planted on the floor: right and left sides of the balls of the foot, and right and left sides of the heels. Conversely, you can use the metaphor of a car and ask students to feel all four "wheels" of each foot firmly grounded.

2. Draw participants' attention to the sense of groundedness. They might sway from side to side, front to back and then resettle in stillness. Ask them to close their eyes.
3. Next, have them draw their attention from that sense of groundedness to a sense of energy that is animating the tissues of their legs. Their ankles are steady and balanced, their calves holding them firmly. Ask them to draw up on their knee caps or place a very slight bend in their knees (to avoid locking the knees backward for those who are prone to hyperextension). Have them feel the strength of their thigh muscles.
4. Then, bring their awareness to the pelvis, asking them to draw the tailbone down, which will help realign the lower back. Ask them to imagine creating space between the hip bones and the lower rib cage, which lengthens and firms the lower torso.
5. From here, participants can be instructed to imagine space between each of their ribs, and to lift the sternum at the center of the breastbone, creating more space for the lungs to expand. Here is a good point to remind them to take deep inhalations and full exhalations, filling and emptying the more-expansive lungs.
6. Have them draw the shoulders back and melt the shoulder blades down. Ask them to relax their arms and hands and lengthen the neck, drawing the crown of the head upward and *slightly* tucking the chin so that the back of the neck is lengthened and drawn into alignment with the rest of the spine.
7. Have participants breathe here for several rounds of breath, tuning into the sensations of energy flow in the body as they've brought it back into a vibrant posture. See if they can find the energy within this stillness.

When the time feels right, have participants take their seats. A few moments could be invested in discussing the experience of mountain pose before the conversation resumes.

Accommodations

Ask those who remain seated to draw their awareness to each part of the body you mention, imagining that they are sending energy and openness to each area as their awareness touches it. Those without movement in their legs, for example, might imagine the flow of blood into these areas of the body and then participate in the movements of the torso, shoulders, and neck if that is within their ability.

MIND

Witness: Agent

Meditation and mindfulness cultivate the perspective of the witness, that part of ourselves that observes without judgment. When we speak of the nonjudgmental awareness that is mindfulness, we are speaking of the witness perspective. So mindfulness exercises, from mindful speaking and listening to breath awareness and noting the pause between breaths, enhance our ability to engage with the witness within. The exercise of witness: agent calls on us to inhabit these roles consciously as we practice, moving "out" to witness emotions, thoughts, and behavior before moving back "in," interacting as conscious agents of our actions. This exercise is also known as thought labeling, and it can help practitioners to become aware of habitual thought patterns or "runaway" thoughts that take us outside of the present moment.

To Practice:

1. In a comfortable position and a place that is relatively free from distractions, begin to observe your thoughts: *I'm hungry. What will I make for dinner tonight? Do I need to stop by the grocery store? I wish I didn't have to cook and clean up too.* As with other mindfulness exercises, an objective is nonjudgmental awareness, which means witnessing the thoughts without critique and then letting them go. I like to use the metaphor of a leaf falling from the tree: each thought is a leaf, but I'm not going to catch it. I'm going to let the breeze carry it away.

   This observation is a complete mindfulness exercise on its own. But taking the step of labeling thoughts before releasing them can help you identify what you think about, which is particularly helpful if you're trying to break the habit of a particular thought pattern.

2. Labeling thoughts can be done in a number of ways.
   a. Useful versus not useful thoughts: *Is this constructive? Is it destructive?* Label and then let the thought go.
   b. Type of thought: *This is fearing. This is planning. This is remembering. This is judging.* Label and then let go.
   c. Sensation: *This thought makes me feel constriction in my chest. This thought makes me clench my fists. This makes me feel hot. This makes my throat tight.* Notice and then let go.
   d. Emotion: *This thought makes me happy. Fearful. Sad. Angry. Annoyed.* Notice then let go.

Each time we label or annotate our thoughts in this way, we engage the witness within. Rather than allowing the thoughts to dictate our reactions, we become more conscious agents who can choose constructive actions and words when we return to interacting with others.

This exercise can be practiced on a regular basis, regardless of where one is. In a group setting, it might be helpful to ask participants to periodically engage in this exercise during conversation. The more they are able to witness what is going on with their thoughts, the more they will be able to choose the responses they want to offer in any given moment. This is also what we practice when we ask for a "temperature check" at the end of a conversation. When we circle the room and ask participants for a one- or two-word adjective that describes their current state, we as asking them to label their thoughts and/or feelings.

Walking Talks

Moving in same direction is an embodied practice that enhances cooperation and consensus. Rather than being face-to-face with someone and thus embodying an oppositional stance, walking talks enable participants to move forward toward the same destination, literalizing the path to a shared goal. In classes, I've presented a question or topic for discussion and asked pairs of students to leave the classroom and take a walk together, answering the question or discussing the topic for a specified amount of time before they return. This exercise has offered a number of benefits in addition to allowing students a shared goal. Time outside the classroom, specifically in nature, has given students new perspectives on a topic that might feel stagnant in the classroom. In asking students to move outside of our classroom space, I'm also offering them an opportunity to be inspired by the new sights and sounds that will surround them. We all know that "stepping away" from a problem for a time can bring us new perspective; similarly, the new perspective of a space outside the classroom has helped students approach a topic with fresh insights. This is also a great exercise for bringing fresh energy into a class. If the average maximum adult attention span is 20 minutes, then offering a change of scenery, not to mention the blood flow of movement, can really spur a renewal of energy for conversation and engagement with others in the classroom.

Accommodations

For students needing special accommodations, this exercise can be modified easily. The objective is to change the scenery and encourage new movements, so even asking students to sit together facing a window may be enough. Asking students to move consciously, perhaps through deep diaphragmatic breathing, can increase oxygenation of the blood and encourage alertness in the brain. Or you might ask for amplified movements of the body, leading students in several rounds of deep inhalations as they reach their arms overhead and then full exhalations as they bring their palms together in front of the heart.

Online Alternative: Mindful Seeing

Those in online classrooms can be taught the practice of mindful seeing. Although this isn't an exercise for paired discussion or question answering, it does offer fresh perspective and interrupt the narrative patterns of judgment and labeling that can be our default state.

1. Move near a window (or even outside if you give this as an asynchronous assignment).
2. The objective is to look without labeling. Instead of thinking "bird" or "tree," pay attention to colors, textures, patterns, and the play of light and shadow.
3. Pay attention to movement, to shapes, to the physical realities being witnessed, even working to see them as if for the first time.
4. Observe without critique, and be aware without fixating on a thought or following a narrative.
5. If you become distracted, notice again.

After a specified amount of time, ask participants to return to the group. It can be helpful to point out the worthwhile applications of this exercise: the more we practice observing without critique, looking without labeling, the more we can bring this skill to bear on interpersonal interactions. Imagine being able to interrupt the automated biases that color our view of others and the world. Imagine being able to listen to different perspectives without fixating on our judgment of them as wrong or the narrative we would like to share when it's our turn to speak. This nonjudgmental observation of reality—even the reality that someone else thinks differently than we do—is a beneficial skill for difficult conversations and for living in diverse community.

SPIRIT

Counting Breath

We can count the breaths to achieve a specific state of energy—longer inhalations for increased vitality, longer exhales for a sense of relaxation. Guide participants in the former when energy seems to be waning and in the latter if tensions increase and conversation becomes heated.

To Practice

1. Instruct participants to sit up straight in their chairs, lengthening their spines and drawing their shoulders back and down, as they would in mountain pose.
2. Explain that you will begin by counting to a specific number as they inhale, perhaps six, and that you'd like them to match the length of their breath to the count you give. You will give them a shorter count to which they can match their exhalation—for example, "Take a deep inhalation for the count of one, two, three, four, five, six. Pause. Exhale for four, three, two, one. Inhale." You might mention that when they pause, they can note the space of stillness between breaths. This is a moment of mindfulness, where they can briefly notice "being present" rather than "being active."
3. Count for several rounds and then ask them to continue the count in their heads.
4. Instruct them when to conclude, releasing the exercise at the end of an exhalation.

Before returning to conversation, ask students to note how they feel. Have they increased their sense of energy (with the longer inhalations) or begun to relax (with the longer exhalations)? Have them sit with this feeling, tuning into any new sensations in the body and the quality of their breathing.

CONSTRUCTIVE CONVERSATION APPLICATIONS

When are these exercises most appropriate during a conversation? When they're going to return students to the beneficial practices established for difficult conversations. Are two students rabidly disagreeing? Would it be useful to pair those students in a walking talk, asking the class a question that will open a new avenue of exploration within their oppositional perspectives? (The oppositional students will certainly feel uncomfortable, but they shouldn't feel unsafe with each other.) Are tensions in the classroom too high and does it seem like a path forward has been blocked? Guide students in extending their exhalations, having them imagine releasing tension from specific parts of the body as they exhale. Or have students pause for a witness: agent practice when they seem at a stalemate. Guide them through a body scan and thought labeling; simply checking in with their bodies and identifying their emotion-based thought patterns can introduce a new awareness of how they can productively re-enter conversation with others.

HUMAN BEINGS DOING: MINDFULNESS IN EVERYDAY LIFE

All of the mindfulness and movement practices described here can be engaged individually as we go about our daily lives. The witness: agent exercise can be engaged whenever we like and wherever we find ourselves. We can practice while driving in a car and feeling agitated by traffic. We can practice when we're having a conversation over dinner, cleaning the dishes, or mowing the lawn. We can practice mindful seeing when we first wake in the morning or when we're feeling distracted at a work meeting, bringing our awareness back to the present moment. We can stand in mountain pose when we've been in front of the computer and need to engage our bodies for a moment. We can suggest a walk with a friend or partner when we're having a disagreement. The more we notice when these practices can be engaged in daily life, the more likely we are to be aware of their usefulness in difficult conversations.

Chapter 3

From Page to Presence
Using Literary Studies to Engage the World

MINDFUL OF STORIES

In her self-reflection at the end of our Black American Literature class on race and citizenship, my student Dee (pseudonym) wrote that, she was unlike the black characters in the few books of African American literature she'd read for previous classes:

> I am not the unaccepting, closed-minded black father figure. I am not the brave little girl walking up the steps to a segregated school. I am not a civil rights activist yelling in the streets. I am not the brave teenager whose brother/father/uncle/what-have-you sells drugs in the street to make ends meet for my single mother. I am, however, a black young adult with an imagination. I am the try hard, I am the "eloquent," "well-spoken for a black girl" black person.
>
> Through this class and the works we've read in it, I've been able to understand my blackness deeper. There was no innate fault in my blackness, just as there is something innately black about my writing . . . I avoided black authors on the incorrect notion that black literature was innately incorrect and poor quality due to my continued schooling in predominantly white institutions that, knowingly or not, excluded black authors and creators from the curriculum. Blackness and the written word in this course were linked in a way I had never considered. There were writers writing about their own experience with blackness, ethnicity, and how they intertwine. There were writers writing about characters whose blackness was not in question, it is plain to see, and they were people. They weren't the black friend or the black lover. They were the friend who happened to be black. They were the lover who happened to be black.

Dee's comments make clear that stories matter. They matter individually for readers who, like Dee, see or don't see themselves within them. They matter as we navigate our individual place in the larger world and in our smaller communities. They help us belong. They distinguish us from others, and they unite us with those we'd imagined as different from ourselves. They matter collectively for groups that make sense of their pasts and shape their futures for, as Jerome Bruner states "cultures rely upon narrative conventions to maintain their coherence and to shape their members to their requirements" (Bruner 2010, 45). Stories shape us even as we shape them. And because of their importance to our individual and collective identities, stories deserve our mindful attention.

HOW WILL WE BE? LITERATURE AND THE EMPATHIC IMAGINATION

Years ago, I taught a class that I called "Literature and the Empathic Imagination." The class reminded students that we can look to literature superficially for entertainment or more deeply for its ability to illuminate life and provide us with windows into diverse experiences. Through exposing ourselves to other ways of being in the world, we can spark our empathic imagination, increasing our awareness of and emotional response to realities far different from our own. Our reading explored literature that was meant to help us answer the question "How will we be?" and by that I meant for students to ask themselves not only who they are but also how they intended to be in relationship to others and in community with others. The texts were selected to help us delve empathically into others' experiences in order that we question how people in various contexts choose to structure their lives; what is privileged; and what values—both conscious and unconscious—are used to shape lives, relationships, and communities. By extension, our exploration allowed for self-reflection on how we wanted to go about forming our own lives, relationships, and communities.

We began with the American Transcendentalists—namely Emerson and Thoreau—but through our semester together, we also moved backward in time, reading works that had inspired those American writers. We read *The Bhagavad Gita*. We read from the *Yoga Sutras* of Patanjali. We read these and other books as wisdom texts from various spiritual and philosophical traditions, highlighting what they shared regarding *how* one is to live, both individually and communally.

Of course, one need not read exclusively from an American canon or the world's wisdom traditions in order to gain clues about how to live life, how to interact with others, what causes conflict, and what restores harmony.

Literature, or stories in general, touch our imaginations and, when we let them, can spark our empathy—our mental and emotional understanding of another or a situation. Likewise, the literature we read can give us insight into our own identities and experiences, often allowing us to view ourselves with more kindness and compassion.

Empathy is rooted in compassion for another. It is feeling *with*, rather than feeling *for*—it is both cognitive in that we imagine another's perspective and affective in that we imagine another's feelings. Suzanne Keen describes empathy as a "vicarious, spontaneous sharing of affect" (Keen 2006, 208). It entails broadening one's perspective and applying mindfulness (nonjudgmental awareness) to another's experience. Keen notes that empathy can be sparked by "witnessing another's emotional state, by hearing about another's condition, or even by reading" and that it entails "mirroring what a person might be expected to feel in that condition or context" (Keen 2006, 208). Practicing empathy in conversation involves constructive communication skills, rather than critique, and thus can be facilitated through mindfulness techniques. Practices that help us visit and "realize" another's perspective can develop this mindfully rooted skill of empathy, so listening to (and reading) others' stories is a valuable practice for increasing our ability to empathize.

Why do we need stories, though? And what purposes do they serve? In the article "Why Stories Matter," Marshall Ganz writes that a challenge for leaders who want to spark change is "figur[ing] out how to break through the inertia of habit to get people to pay attention" (Ganz 2009, n.p.). Most people like to be entertained, and stories entertain us. They also enlighten and inspire, and they can be a catalyst for our creativity and change. Stories possess the ability to help make complex situations, emotions, and realities both understandable and relatable, and they tap into our "unthinking" selves. Ganz states:

> A story communicates fear, hope, and anxiety, and because we can feel it, we get the moral not just as a concept, but as a teaching of our hearts. That's the power of story. That's why most of our faith traditions interpret themselves as stories, because they are teaching our hearts how to live as choiceful human beings capable of embracing hope over fear, self-worth and self-love over self-doubt, and love over isolation and alienation. (Ganz 2009, n.p.)

When we mindfully approach stories—either in literature or in life—we make a conscious choice to engage with them at this deeper level of meaning. After all, "We don't just talk about hope and other values in abstractions. We talk about them in the language of stories because stories are what enable us to communicate these values to one another" (Ganz 2009, n.p.). And although not all people respond positively to studying literature, most can be engaged through storytelling, which is why individual voices expressed through stories are a powerful avenue toward understanding and empathy.

Deborah Schiffrin and Anna De Fina note "Narratives are fundamental to our lives. We dream, plan, complain, endorse, entertain, teach, learn, and reminisce by telling stories. They provide hopes, enhance or mitigate disappointments, challenge or support moral order, and test out theories of the world at both personal and communal levels" (Schiffrin and De Fina 2010, n.p.). Once we recognize stories' value in these ways, we teachers can then consider how we can help students approach narratives mindfully, especially those narratives that challenge our preconceptions of the world or our fundamental beliefs about life and ourselves. How do we engage with narratives that are vastly different from our own life stories, or the stories we tell of our own lives? And how do we encourage mindful reading that builds the empathic imagination of students and fosters their empathic engagement?

In *A Writer's Guide to Mindful Reading*, literacy scholar Ellen Carillo recommends mindful reading practices: "Reading mindfully means paying attention not just to the content of the text—what it says—but rather to the process of reading itself by adjusting how you read based on what the piece asks of you" (Carillo 2017, vi). So, if we're asking our students to engage their empathic imaginations through reading, we might suggest mindfulness techniques that call on them not only to fully encounter their own emotional and relational responses to a text—traditionally the domain of reader response theories of literary criticism—but also to engage with the text through questions that increase their sense of curiosity about another's experience and that, at times, call on them to imagine themselves in that other experience. The Metta meditation offered in this chapter's mindfulness and movement practices section works to build empathy and, in much the same way, we can call on students to draw on their deep emotional responses to what they read by imagining relationships with fictional characters or by drawing parallels between fictional characters and real people that students know and love.

Because our ways of reading are related to our ways of listening, teachers and discussion facilitators who encourage deep and active listening can liken this to mindful reading. *How are we reading?* is the question to ask, just as we would ask *How are we listening?* As with listening, we can encourage deep and critical reading. This critical eye is not negative but is questioning, probing, and encouraging of "if . . . then" thinking. If what I'm reading is so different from my own experience, and if it is true, then what will I choose to do? Readers can be encouraged in a dialogue with the texts they read, asking questions and considering how the narratives they're reading prompt their evaluations of the world and their own place within it.

In delineating her theory of narrative empathy, Suzanne Keen states, "Character identification often invites empathy, even when the fictional character and reader differ from one another in all sorts of practical and obvious ways, but empathy for fictional characters appears to require only minimal elements of identity, situation, and feeling, not necessarily complex or realistic characterization" (Keen 2006, 214). Our ability to empathize with nonhuman characters in films, for example—whether they are animals, robots, or aliens—points to the truth of Keen's argument and reminds us that we need not identify with a character—or a real person— in order to express empathy for them. Requiring students to engage with characters who don't share their identities is a useful avenue for cultivating understanding of and empathy for those who are different, reinforcing the importance of sharing underrepresented narratives with all populations of students.

We can use this type of fictional engagement as a precursor to community engagement, the subject of chapter 4, allowing students to build empathy skills and the desire for social action. C. Daniel Baston has proposed a link between empathy and altruism, and many scholars have issued the claim that "empathy leads to altruistic action," offering "arguments for cultivating novel reading as an empathic activity that could make us better world citizens" (Levin 2016, 188). Other scholars, such as Amy Coplan, however, note that altruism may be rooted in sympathy, rather than empathy: "Just as I can sympathize with another without trying to imagine the world from her perspective, I can also empathize with another without experiencing concern for her well-being" (Coplan 2004, 145). Coplan cites research that emphasizes the "self-other differentiation" involved in empathy, which "enables the empathizer to observe the boundaries of the other as well as his- or herself and to respect the singularity of the other's experience as well as his or her own" (Coplan 2004, 144). This boundary recognition distinguishes empathy from emotional contagion, wherein the observer "catches" the feelings of another as if they were his or her own, rather than *imaginatively* engaging those feelings.

But imaginatively engaging with feelings and ideas is the realm and magic of story. Stories imaginatively place us in other experiences, identities, and worlds and our mindful engagement with them can foster empathic recognition, helping us understand others—and ourselves—more fully. Empathic recognition functions on the boundary between self and other, highlighting the fact that empathy is other-focused: "In order to successfully empathize, I must not confuse what *I* would experience with what *the target* experiences so I must be careful not to let aspects of my own characterization influence the central imaginative task" (Coplan 2004, 146). When we hear (or read) stories, we imagine the perspective of the other person (or character) and imagine his or her emotional state, which—coupled with compassion and concern—can lead us to our own desires for the well-being of that person. In so doing, we encounter ourselves—our own desires being fueled by who we feel ourselves to be and the values we hold.

Stories about others foster this empathic recognition and self-reflection. In addition to engaging students in reading others' stories, we can choose to encourage students and other discussion participants to share their own stories, building opportunities for additional self-reflection and engagement with others across boundaries of difference. As in any personal conversation, storytelling requires participants to feel safe and respected beforehand. Students and others who engage in storytelling need to trust each other—and the facilitator. This is a foundation that needs to be built from the first encounter, as discussed at length in chapter 2. Given that some people are more reserved than others, preferring to remain observers rather than vocal discussion participants, multiple avenues for storytelling should be offered. People can speak in class. They can write personal reflections (which needn't always be shared with the class or even the facilitator). They can create visual representations of the stories they want to share. They can use social media and other digital avenues to share their "voices" more publicly.

Just as there are multiple ways to tell stories, storytelling can have various prompts. Often, a book my class is reading will prompt students to share the way the narrative resonates with their own lives, and they begin to tell personal stories in response. Sometimes, outrage and righteous anger prompt storytelling, as was the case with the stories of Sikh and Muslim Americans collected by Valarie Kaur in the wake of 9/11. In my own classes, current events often cause outrage in students and demand that we pause the syllabus calendar in order to make sense of our world through collective sharing of and response to these stories.

Sometimes a teacher's question or assignment will encourage stories, as my "Who Am I? Personal Statement" assignment encourages my students to share their personal anecdotes. I use this assignment when I teach Black American Literature, and it consists of a personal reflection on the meanings and manifestations of race in students' own lives. Even students who have never considered race a salient point of their identity are tasked with understanding how and why this can be so. This "Who Am I?" racial reflection has inspired profound storytelling on the part of students, so much so that I asked one class to share their stories in a podcast we created—20/20 Voices—which highlighted students' own sense of identity, issuing out of the stories they had told (and had been told) about their own lives.

UNTOLD STORIES

It's clear that telling stories helps us understand our own experiences, our own lives, and our own identities. Taking the social constructionist approach to identity development, some scholars have investigated how we build our identities through language. Malavika Shetty, for example, has conceptualized identity as an "interactional accomplishment, produced and negotiated in discourse. Identities, in this approach, are thus not stable and independent of language but are constantly negotiated in the course of [dialogic and narrative] interactions" (Shetty 2010, 97). Identities, then, are not "*a priori* categories that exist apart from particular interactions. . . . They are not merely represented in discourse but also [are] performed, enacted, and embodied" through narratives (Shetty 2010, 97). We construct our identities in part through the stories we tell about ourselves and to ourselves, and we affiliate with identity groups through such narratives as well, telling ourselves stories about others' similarities to or differences from ourselves. As "identity is often seen as emerging from the twin concepts of similarity and difference," social groups are organized around our ideas of sameness and divergence, which come to us through the stories we tell—even unconsciously, as when we see a person's skin color and link it to the narratives we've heard about it (Shetty 2010, 98). This process is immediate and often unrecognized, demonstrating the deep-rootedness of story in our subconscious minds and the way in which we use these "untold" stories to organize our lives. As Bruner notes, "Contemporary common sense is increasingly taking the view that 'realities' are made, not found—the constructivist view. The dichotomy of 'truth versus fiction' is becoming less dichotomous. More latterly, indeed, we have even become interested in how narrative creates its realities" (Bruner 2010, 47).

The ubiquitous nature of this process highlights its importance and calls on those who teach and facilitate discussions to help students and participants recognize the stories they have been told, that they continue to tell themselves, and that they proceed to tell publicly. Bringing reflection to bear on the stories we've been told about our identities and those of others is part of how we can answer the question "How will we be?" with clarity and consciousness. Bringing mindful attention to these processes of storytelling allows us to determine which stories we want to retain and which we are better off discarding. Mindfulness also allows us to become aware of the stories that have shaped our own identities and whether these stories are worthy of who—and how—we intend to be.

Narrative empathy is an avenue toward increased awareness of others and an increased desire to compassionately engage with them. Thus, underrepresented narratives—broadly conceived but also local, personal, and intergenerational—are essential to developing one's ability to empathize and engage with diverse populations. Typically, underrepresented narratives are imagined as those from minority groups—people of color, women, LGBTQ+—because for so long the Western literary canon has been dominated by white cisgender male authors. Expanding literary canons to include these underrepresented groups is essential, and we can also consider other sources of underrepresented stories. What stories and populations have locally been undervalued? What personal stories might be resurrected in our own families? What do older generations have to share and, in listening, what can we learn?

For several semesters, I've had my Black American Literature and African Diaspora classes delve deeply into the local histories of African Americans in our city of Jacksonville, Florida. Valuing the expertise of a local writer, architect, and urban planner Ennis Davis, we've taken bike rides through a historically black part of our downtown, listening to him tell stories of the important events that took place and lives that originated here. Harriet Tubman led reconnaissance missions against the Confederate army here. James Weldon Johnson was born here. Cab Calloway and Ma Rainey sang here, and Ray Charles lived here. Exposing students to these histories through the stories Ennis tells brings these histories to life, enlivens the students, and helps them value this city in new ways. They also become engaged in wanting to share these stories with others. In particular, those students who want to become teachers themselves feel fired up to make these histories known to future generations and to hold our city accountable for recognizing, valuing, and celebrating its diversity. This is the power of stories.

The genre of Afrofuturism is one example of raised consciousness toward the stories we've been told and those we wish to begin telling. Although the genre existed long before Mark Dery coined the term in 1994, Afrofuturism has been defined as "speculative fiction that treats African-American themes and addresses African-American concerns in the context of twentieth-century technoculture—and, more generally, African-American signification that appropriates images of technology and a prosthetically enhanced future" (Dery 1994, 180). Prior to this definition, authors were already contending with the genre's central question: "Can a community whose past has been deliberately rubbed out, and whose energies have subsequently been consumed by the search for legible traces of its history, imagine possible futures?" (Dery 1994, 180). The genre emerged out of the erasure of African American stories (an erasure that continues contemporarily), the need to tell an inclusive history, and the essential task of narrating oneself into the future. The erasure of nondominant stories has been coupled with narratives that relegate nondominant cultures to the past (consider the myths of the "vanishing Indian" or the "noble savage" who must leave his uncivilized past behind or be left in the past himself). Thus, speaking oneself into the future is a mindful and revolutionary act, one that demands awareness of how identities will resist erasure and be carried forward. Whether dystopian or utopian, this future is narrated in order to insist on one's right to be. Such narratives are acts of resistance, reclamation, and renewal. They are narratives that demand the stories unimagined and untold by the dominant culture be recognized. Irvine and Gal have described "erasure" as a semiotic "process of selectively ignoring variations." In this process, "differences regarded by the dominant ideology of a group to be inconsequential are either discounted or ignored" (Irvine and Gal 2000, 38). Afrofuturism and other genres like it demand that these discounted, ignored, or formerly untold stories be told. Thus, "[Narrative] not only shapes our ways of communicating with each other and our ways of experiencing the world, but it also gives form to what we imagine, to our sense of what is possible. With its aid, we pole vault beyond the presently expectable. And of course it shapes our conceptions of the past" (Bruner 2010, 45). Those who write such narratives effectively write a more inclusive story of the past and write themselves into the future, insisting on the generative and regenerative power of storytelling.

FROM PAGE TO PRESENCE

Stories help us reorder the past, make sense of the present, and generate possibilities for the future. They build an understanding of the self, either through the telling of one's own stories or the recognition of one's self in another's stories, and thus they help build communities. Regardless of the academic discipline or organizational purpose, digging into stories leads us to unearth the richness in our own individual and communal soil. In a literature classroom, we move from discussions of stories as texts to stories as life. In other disciplines, stories help disparate individuals build group cohesion. They tell us (and others) who we are and where we belong. Guajardo et. al. note "Stories matter because they help us build and sustain relationships. Stories matter because they inform us about place. And stories matter because they help us see possibilities and hope beneath layers of despair. They help us find courage when we are frightened. And stories help us find agency when we feel powerless" (Guajardo et. al. 2016, 19). Storytelling becomes a key component of these researchers' Community Learning Exchanges (CLEs), which they describe as an opportunity to "invest in our relationships, recognize our gifts, explore our stories, respect our place" (Guajardo et. al. 2016, 5). As their work demonstrates, the CLE is a pedagogical model for self-reflection, community building, and tapping into the wisdom of one's community. By coming together to tell their stories and share their thoughts on a given topic, participants in a CLE inquire about their communal assets, tap into their communal wisdom, and find avenues toward communal empowerment and progress.

Storytelling and listening mindfully to others' stories help us apply various answers to the question *How will we be?*, to imagine scenarios and test various responses in our own imaginations. We then move from imagined responses to what we read on the page to making conscious choices about our presence in the world. How will we be? We imagine. We decide. We act. Stories facilitate this shift from page to presence. We need stories because they inspire. They create. They cause. They build. "We turn to stories and pictures and music because they show us who and what and why we are, and what our relationship is to life and death, what is essential, and what . . . will not burn" (L'Engle 1972, 120). When we're mindful, reflection on others' stories leads us to curiosity and wonder about their lives, sometimes to deep concern and righteous anger, often to a sense of connection when we realize what we share—even with those we perceive as different. The qualities of curiosity, concern, and connection may then propel us to broader community engagement, the subject of chapter 4.

Mindfulness and Movement Practices

*BODY

Note: Always use extreme caution when beginning or facilitating a new movement practice. Practitioners may be advised to consult a medical professional or trained movement specialist before attempting specific body-based practices. Facilitators should remind practitioners that they must not move in any way that will be injurious or cause pain.

Standing Back Bend

Because empathy is emotional, feeling *with* someone, we might imagine it as rooted in the heart. Metaphysically (or metaphorically) speaking, we can imagine that heart-focused practices may help us create the emotional openness to expand our capacity for empathy. For this reason, I recommend *asanas* that are "heart-openers." These postures are backbends, which open the front of the body and strengthen the back. This is a perfect metaphor for empathy, as remaining open to others' emotional realities demands courage (a strong backbone) in us.

There are many ways to practice backbends, from simple seated exercises to those that are practiced standing or even on the belly. In addition to the cat/cow pose detailed in the mindfulness and movement practices from chapter 1, I will describe a standing backbend here.

To Practice

1. Begin in mountain pose (see chapter 2 mindfulness and movement practices).

2. Feel grounded in the feet and strong through the legs. On an inhalation, raise the arms overhead, straightening the arms and facing the palms toward each other. (Depending on the openness of the shoulders—and space in the room—the arms can be raised by moving them forward and up or out to the sides. If there is pain in the shoulders, neck, or lower back, the arms can be kept in a V shape or slightly forward of the body. Remind participants to move in ways that feel right for their own bodies.)
3. If it will be comfortable to do so, lift the chin and tilt the head up and back. If this causes pain in the neck, then lift just the gaze, drawing the eyes upward.
4. Continuing to root and stabilize in the lower body, keep the legs strong and the belly firm. Inhale and sense the spine lengthening, exhale, and reach the fingertips up and back (if this is physically accessible) while continuing to lift the gaze.
5. Breathe here for three to five full breaths, paying attention to the sensations in the body and discontinuing anything that feels painful (sharp and electrical).
6. On an inhalation, feel the heart lifting as you bring the spine back into a neutral upright position. Exhale and lower the arms back to the sides.

Backbends are energizing since they create expanse in the front body, allowing us to breathe more fully into the lungs. Check in after this practice to see if you do, indeed, feel an increase of energy, lightness of spirit, and receptivity of heart.

Accommodations

This pose can also be practiced near a wall if one feels unsteady or seated if standing isn't an option. If a wall is used, then position the body not more than an arm's length from it before turning one's back to the wall. This allows one to reach the fingertips toward the wall behind, creating a deeper sense of stability. If seated, one might, shift to the front of the seat and practice the movements from the waist up. If the raised arm movement isn't accessible, then one can draw the shoulders back and down while pressing the sternum forward and up. On an inhalation, imagine a balloon inflating the front of the chest and see what subtle movements might shift the front of the body.

MIND

Metta Meditation

Metta is the Buddhist loving-kindness meditation, which is said to open the doors and windows to the heart and transform us. It is also said to be an antidote to fear, which stifles the connection that might be possible between ourselves and others.

To Practice

1. First, close your eyes. Visualize yourself in a protective bubble, surrounded by radiant light and filled with all the qualities you consider virtuous—perhaps love, forgiveness, compassion, wisdom, generosity, abundance, and healing. Into this circle of light, you will sequentially call in five beings and offer each this simple wish: *May you be free from suffering.*
2. First being: Yourself—this can be hard for many, but learning to love ourselves is beneficial and important, even essential. *May you be free from suffering.*
3. Second being: Someone You Love—family, friends, lovers, even animals or nature can serve as the second being. The point is to experience a tangible sensation of love for this being—most people feel it in the heart region—so pick the being that gives you the strongest sensation of love. *May you be free from suffering.*
4. Third being: Someone You Do Not Like—This may be someone you have had conflict with or are currently having conflict with; it may even be someone you don't know who nevertheless makes you angry (like a politician). *May you be free from suffering.* (And try to mean it!)
5. Fourth being: A Stranger—This might be someone in the room with you now whom you do not know, someone you passed by in your car today, a stranger in the grocery store. This is just someone you don't know and never speak to. Call an image of this person to mind and say, *May you be free from suffering.*
6. Fifth being: All of Earth—Here, visualize all of the Earth and every being it holds—humans, stones, plants, animals, and so on. Visualize the Earth as vibrant and pristine. It is clean and healthy with clear waters and mountains abundant with strong trees. *May you be free from suffering.*

When you are ready, open your eyes and tune into your thoughts and feelings. Was the practice uncomfortable? Liberating? Touching? Maddening? Sit with that reality for a time.

Metta is simple on paper but can be quite complex in practice. And it is a practice. Like any practice, the more energy and attention we give to it, the more it can transform us and our ways of seeing and being in the world and being in relation to others. The more it can help us practice arête (an ancient Greek concept of living up to one's full potential) in the everyday.

SPIRIT

Expanded Heart Breath

This breath exercise increases our awareness of the heart, figuratively a seat of empathy. It helps us imagine an increased capacity within it for empathic recognition of others and helps us release the constrictions and tensions that diminish our capacity to respond to others' feelings.

To Practice

1. Sit in a comfortable, upright position or lie down.
2. Begin with deep belly breathing, inhaling to expand the belly away from the spine and exhaling to draw it back.
3. After three rounds of belly breathing, draw your awareness to the center of your chest and imagine your heart; you might see a Valentine's Day shape or imagine the anatomical organ. With your next deep inhalation, imagine your breath moving into your heart and suffusing it with a warm red or soft pink light. As you exhale fully, imagine that light pushing out smudgy smoke from your heart center.
4. With each inhalation as the light enters your heart, imagine your heart gradually growing in size. With each exhalation of smoke, you make more room for your heart to expand.
5. Continue this meditative breath exercise for several rounds of breath.
6. Releasing control of the breath, return to normal breathing, keeping your awareness at your heart center. (You might still imagine that red or pink color suffusing the area.) Feel if there is more ease and less constriction in your chest.
7. Try to maintain this sense of expansive openness as you return to your activities.

CONSTRUCTIVE CONVERSATION APPLICATIONS

I recommend the practices in this section before a demanding conversation. When teachers plan to introduce an emotionally challenging or potentially conflict-laden subject, they might ask students to practice expanded heart breath or Metta. Of course, as with any of the practices, teachers can also feel free to pause an increasingly tense conversation for mindful release of constriction from the body and emotions. Additionally, the backbend exercise might be especially useful at the end of a challenging conversation and before students are released from class, helping them feel open again after conversations that might have caused them to retreat into themselves.

HUMAN BEINGS DOING: MINDFULNESS IN EVERYDAY LIFE

Meditations and physical exercises that help us stay open to life and relationships certainly have a benefit for our daily lives. Whether we feel heated emotions from watching the news, encountering aggressive drivers, or experiencing a family conflict, most of us have experiences that challenge our willingness to stay open to and empathetic with others. Maintaining one or more of these heart-expanding practices on a daily basis will have a noticeable effect on our reactions to the stresses we encounter with others. For example, over time, Metta meditation will help transform habitually negative thoughts about others—even strangers—into more neutral or compassionate ones. We will likely find ourselves maintaining more equanimity in addition to empathy, meeting others with more openness, curiosity, and wonder.

Physical practices that expand the front body will also change our posture. With all of the driving and computer work demanded in our culture, many of us have curved into a posture that thrusts our necks forward and rounds our shoulders. We have overstretched the backs of our necks and shoulders and have tightened our chest muscles. Considered energetically, this posture hides our hearts, closing us off from meeting others with open and courageous hearts. Altering our physical posture—by drawing our shoulders back and down and extending our necks into their healthy, upward position—has an energetic effect on our willingness to meet others without hiding our hearts and tucking into ourselves like turtles. We begin to physically embody the strength, openness, and courage that empathy demands.

Chapter 4

Engaging Community

Recently, my student Drea (pseudonym) asked, "How can I transform the knowledge I acquire from these readings and our discussions from intellectual discourse to real action?" This question is a natural outcome of developing awareness of difference, studying social justice issues, and engaging empathy. The question is implicit in much of what educators teach, whether the subject be social justice specifically or educational pedagogy more generally. Most teachers want to offer their students authentic assignments that will have them developing and practicing practical skills and applying knowledge to real-life situations. Because we don't live in the classroom but in communities, educators want to ensure that what transpires in the classroom can be utilized in students' lives, and this includes the skills necessary for fostering social justice, practical citizenship, and democratic engagement. David Mathews notes, "In a word, democracy is work, and citizens need to know how to do the work that gives them power. The only way they can learn how the work is done is by actually doing it. So academic institutions have to combine classroom experiences with experiences working in communities" (Mathews 2017, n.p.). Our classrooms can become communities—environments that promote constructive conversations—but they are never our primary ones. Fostering student engagement with communities beyond the classroom facilitates student learning, integration of knowledge, and satisfaction, and at its best offers a reciprocal relationship of mutually beneficial exchange between the classroom and the community.

MINDFUL OF PURPOSE

Connecting students with—and recognizing their prior connection to—communities beyond our classroom community is a primary focus of education. Even in disciplines where we're helping students prepare for specific jobs, we are preparing them to connect with and thrive within a given community and in society at large. Drea's question leads us to understand this fundamental but often unexamined purpose of education. Of course, educators are called to become aware of and explicit about their purpose when they develop learning objectives for a class: What is the nature of this particular educational endeavor, and what is my purpose in undertaking it? What do I want students to learn? To cultivate a mindful classroom, educators are also called to gain clarity on how these learning objectives are fostered moment by moment and how students' emotional and physical experiences within a classroom intersect with their intellectual experiences. Awareness of these realities in students—and in ourselves as educators—helps foster a mindful classroom and holistic learning environment. Additionally, gaining clarity on one's larger educational beliefs and purposes can help educators, discussion facilitators, and students approach educational spaces mindfully and with clear intentions. Following are some broader educational ideas that are worth exploring before embarking on the collaboration of education:

- Knowledge
  How do you understand knowledge? Is it passed on by others, created in community, arising out of intuition? I typically take a phenomenological approach to the idea of knowledge, believing that we know mainly through experience, which is why community-based, active learning is important in my teaching.
- Learning
  What does it mean to learn? Is application of what one learns necessary, making learning fundamentally about skills acquisition? Is it the acquisition or creation of new knowledge, new abilities, new avenues of thought? And, of course, how is one to ensure that learning is happening?
- Teaching
  What does it mean to teach? Who is a teacher? To my mind, teaching revolves around the asking of good, thought-provoking questions that allow others to develop critical thinking skills, new insights, and new connections among ideas. In the classroom, I recognize that students also have much to teach others (and themselves). Much of what I can do—in addition to sharing expertise—is develop the context for this sharing to happen. Mindful, constructive conversations are at the heart of teaching.

- Curriculum
  What constitutes the curriculum (or curricula) in a given class? What are the desired goals of an individual class/conversation and how does that class propel the goals of the course as a whole? Curricula for conversation-based classes can be specific, with measurable outcomes in mind, but they also should be organic and flexible, allowing numerous avenues to a desired destination. With that destination in mind, the curriculum becomes a map for teaching and learning.
- Education
  What constitutes education, and where does it happen? Education is the realm of learning (and teaching), and it can take place beyond schooling, as the successes of community-based learning attest. (Schooling is based in curricula, but education needn't be.) It can be formal or informal, planned or unplanned, can involve human teachers or not. Still, when it is formal, it is an opportunity to be challenged and therefore an opportunity to grow.

Taking time to mindfully answer such questions is a reflective exercise that allows insight into educators' and students' goals. Discussing these early can also foster an environment of collaboration that respects students' needs and desires for their own education, cultivating not only mindfulness but a sense of community within the classroom.

MINDFUL OF COMMUNITY

Of course, mindfulness happens in the moment, but in a broader sense creating a mindful classroom takes planning and intention on the educator's part. As we cultivate mindful relationships with students and a mindful classroom community, we help them engage with difference and—the more diverse the classroom community—develop cultural competence, a widely popularized term in our increasingly global world. Most classrooms—both face-to-face and online—are ever more diverse, providing opportunities within the classroom for students to learn and practice skills that have real-world benefits for them and the communities of which they are a part. The benefit of cultural competence is obvious for students who seek careers in education, public policy, social work, health care, and other fields that connect workers with the public. Even in more traditional business fields, however, companies find competitive advantage in diversity and in employees who are familiar with and competent in navigating cultural differences, especially since such competence is part of what drives innovation and growth. As a study by Deloitte suggests, "Embracing diversity as a way of thinking is the most effective response for business leaders and an important driver of an organization's innovative engine. When an authentic, inclusive culture is at work, a diverse workforce is capable of producing a range of original and engaging ideas that is simply not possible among homogenous employee populations" ("Diversity" 2021, n.p.).

Global/multicultural fluency is regularly listed in the National Association of Colleges and Employers top-eight competencies employers desire in college graduates. Similarly, according to Rebecca Baer reporting on a recent corporate recruiters' survey:

> Respondents ranked a candidate's ability to fit within an organizational culture the most important trait, followed by the ability to work in teams, and the ability to make an impact. In order to develop these skills and achieve success in a diverse and multicultural workplace, leaders within organizations must possess multi-cultural awareness, knowledge, and skills which allows them to understand and value the ways that culture influences different perceptions of the same problem and solution. Development of Cultural Intelligence allows for the development of one's self-awareness as well so that any assumptions and unconscious biases may come to light and no longer influence decision making in an unintentional way. (Baer 2018, n.p.)

This cultural intelligence and multicultural fluency, then, is as highly valued in the business world as it is in social services sectors, even if this valuation is based on different goals.

But although cultural competence is desired by employers and graduates, another study showed that currently only 18% of employers feel college graduates are well prepared in working with people from different backgrounds ("Falling Short?" 2021, n.p.).

Not only do businesses desire multicultural fluency in employees, but most students also recognize the need to engage competently with difference; value diversity, equity and inclusion; and contribute to social justice causes. According to the Deloitte 2019 Millennial Survey, "Eighty-four percent of traditionally college-aged students consider it their duty to improve the world, and 70% of young people want to find a career that changes the world for the better" ("2019 Millennial Survey"). Nationwide, employment in community and social service occupations is projected to grow 12% from 2019 to 2029, much faster than the average for other occupations, according to the U.S. Bureau of Labor Statistics ("Employment Projections" 2021, n.p.). However, a study by Hart also showed only 21% of college graduates feel well prepared in awareness of diverse cultures in the United States, suggesting more can be done in classrooms to develop this skill in students.

A key way to develop students' multicultural fluency is to engage them in broader and more diverse communities through community-engaged learning opportunities that move students beyond the classroom walls and into interactions with others from diverse backgrounds—in every form diversity takes. These interactions, from dialogues to project collaboration, help develop and translate text- and conversation-based knowledge to real-world applications.

MINDFUL OF CULTURE

Before engaging students in community collaborations, though, it is necessary to help them mindfully explore their preexisting beliefs about their own and others' cultures, especially the cultures with which they'll be asked to engage. A good place to start is to ask students to develop mindfulness about their own minds, their own thinking, by reflecting in a journal on their cultures of origin as well as what they've been taught (or assumed) about other cultures. The opening questions from "Sample Questions for Race-Based Discussion" in chapter 5 can help students begin to think about their understanding of and assumptions about race, and these questions can be tailored to address multiple forms of difference and identity. Then, tapping into diverse perspectives in classroom conversations, developing empathy through reading literature, and generating awareness through media reports on social issues all pave the way for new perspectives and insight. Subsequent student reflections demonstrate their new awareness of cultural difference and their previous assumptions about it.

Educators must also explore their own assumptions and cultural perspectives about difference, being as self-reflective as we ask our students to be. We can share our own developing awareness with students, helping foster a classroom community where everyone feels safe to share. And we can keep our insights in mind as we approach each classroom interaction with mindfulness and intention. As an educator, I try to remember these key points about culture and difference within the classroom and, where appropriate, help students understand these insights as well:

- Appearance isn't always an indicator of culture.
- Cultural competence isn't assured even though diversity is present.
- My awareness of students as human individuals benefits our interactions.
- We model and educate our students on cultural competence through our own interactions with the class.
- Even we instructors (and even those of us in minority positions) bring assumptions and stereotypes into our interactions with others.

- Cultural competence is an ongoing practice that involves self-awareness. We can always become more culturally aware and sensitive, we can continue to be flexible, and we can make adjustments to our courses toward this end.
- Accommodations can usually be made easily, without a great deal of inconvenience to us as instructors, and these accommodations can greatly relieve student stress.

Even those of us who are minority instructors can't forget that cultural competence can always be improved. Each of us has multiple subcultures, and just because I am a minority in one sense doesn't mean that I might not be in the majority in another sense. For example, I am a racial minority, but I am a native English speaker. Thus, I must remain vigilant about my language-based assumptions and work to be inclusive of those who use English as a second language.

One must be self-aware in order to increase cultural competence, so it behooves us to reflect on the ways our cultures shape our experience of and interaction with others. When we do this, our multiple cultures can cease to be a source of conflict or confusion and can add layers of richness and insight to our teaching and learning. As educators, we learn about various student learning styles and abilities. We study pedagogical strategies that help make our courses accessible and available to students. We have considered ways in which the diverse cultural backgrounds of our students have an impact on the class's discussions and perhaps even the content we choose to include. We can also consider the ways in which cultural differences may impact student learning and the ways in which these cultural considerations should be incorporated into our course planning.

For both face-to-face and online classes, educators would do well to consider the way cultural differences can impact our students' learning and interactions, both with us and with their fellow students. Additionally, these cultural considerations may become part of our thinking on fostering accessibility in our courses. Accessibility refers to how available courses are to students of varied physical abilities (sighted or not, hearing impaired or not, etc.) and emotional experiences (are any students suffering from PTSD that might be triggered by our course content?). We can broaden our definition of accessibility to include cultural considerations that may alter individual students' experience of our courses and their content. Because culture impacts behavior, communication, and patterns of thought (Vatrapu 2008, 2–3), it becomes an important consideration for educators as we determine our pedagogical strategies and structure our classes and the conversations therein. Educators must stay mindful of how individual cultures can impact how people learn and even what people think is important to learn. Thus, it is important for educators to pay attention to the ways in which our own cultures, and those of our students, impact teaching and learning, within the classroom and in our community-engaged work.

MINDFUL OF RELATIONSHIPS

Just as we cultivate mindfulness about teaching and learning and about our interpersonal interactions within a classroom, so too must the relationships among students, educators, and community partners be mindfully approached. The goal of community-engaged education is not one-sided, with students extracting knowledge and experience from the community. Instead, the goal is to develop reciprocity, each party offering something of value and gaining something in a mutually beneficial exchange. Such monetary metaphors, though, don't fully convey the full nature of the desired relationship. Ideally, the relationships developed between students and community partners are transformational for both, rather than merely transactional. Enos and Morton see transactional relationships as "often designed to complete short-term tasks. Persons come together on the basis of an exchange, each offering something the other desires. Both benefit from the exchange, and no long-term change is expected" (Enos and Morton 2003, 24). Transformational relationships, on the other hand, are those in which "both [parties] grow and change because of deeper and more sustainable commitments. In a transformational relationship, persons come together in more open-ended processes of indefinite but longer-term duration and bring a receptiveness—if not an overt intention—to explore emergent possibilities, revisit and revise their own goals and identities, and develop systems they work within beyond the status quo" (Enos and Morton 2003, 24).

Given the time constraints of college classes, transactional relationships may seem more easily developed between a given class and a community partner. Yet transformation is also possible, especially if the connections extend throughout a given semester and, potentially, beyond it. Transformative relationships are cultivated, in part, through partnership and collaboration, which are at the heart of community engagement. In fact, the Carnegie Foundation for the Advancement of Teaching defines community engagement as the "collaboration between institutions of higher education and their larger communities (local, regional/state, national, global) for the mutually beneficial exchange of knowledge and resources in a context of partnership and reciprocity." Community engagement emphasizes the inherent knowledge and skills within communities—meaning the students and teacher aren't there to take charge, direct, or control—and looks to the community itself to define its own needs. As artist Rick Lowe has stated, the idea behind community-engaged work is not really to do the work oneself but "to create the platforms and frameworks for people to do the work in their own communities."[1] Furthermore, the community is not seen as an object to be studied or a source to be mined for the one-way benefit of students' knowledge building. When approached in right relationship, community-based learning can be an effective way to develop students' multicultural fluency, to educate them, and to teach them civic responsibility. For community partners, community-based learning can be an opportunity for them to work with young volunteers in meeting community needs. Conversations with community stakeholders before a class commences are essential, as the educator needs to hear the community's needs and collaborate on ways the partnership can benefit the community, not simply the students. Student availability to serve the community in this way is a rewarding experience for both the community and the engaged students, highlighting the mutually beneficial outcomes that can result from collaboration and true partnership.

In the spirit of fostering equal partnership, a number of questions within specific categories[2] should be discussed with the community partners before a class and community project begins:

- Needs: What are the community's needs and what are the needs of the students?
- Benefits of project: Will both parties benefit equally and have growth opportunities because of the project? Will the organizations and institutions be better able to fulfill their purposes because of the relationship?
- Goals and understanding: Do both parties have common goals and mutual understanding regarding these goals, their needs, and their roles?
- Decision making: Are both parties committed to making decisions collaboratively and through consensus? Will both parties invite and encourage each other to express their needs, goals, and roles and to routinely discuss each other's performance?
- Resources: Will both parties contribute resources (of various kinds) to the project? What will these resources be?
- Conflict management: Are both parties willing to deal openly with any conflict, with the shared expectation of reaching a successful resolution?
- Identity: Will this partnership help both parties do the work they need to do and enhance their respective ability to make meaningful contributions?
- Power: How will power be shared equally in this partnership? What will that equal sharing look like?
- Outcomes: Will both parties grow and develop in the fulfillment of their missions? Will regular evaluations of the process occur and improvements be agreed upon?

- Satisfaction: What will enable both parties to be satisfied with the relationship and deem it successful?

Conversations that home in on answers to these questions will help support a truly transformational relationship for both community partners and the students engaged with them, allowing all parties to benefit from and find respect within the relationship.

MINDFUL OF MIND

Community-engaged work benefits from mindfulness—of purpose, communities and cultures, relationships, and mind. Here I return to the topic of mindfulness meditation, of the habit of observing one's thoughts and the ways in which thoughts influence our emotions and our actions. Studying *The Yoga Sutras of Patanjali*, a classic text of the yogic tradition, in my Literature and the Empathic Imagination Class, we read Sutra 33, which imparts this challenge: "By cultivating attitudes of friendliness toward the happy, compassion for the unhappy, delight in the virtuous, and disregard toward the wicked, the mind retains its undisturbed calmness" ("Yoga Sutras" 1978, 54).

When we meet cheerful people, we are drawn toward them and feel cheerful in return. When we encounter those who are suffering, our empathetic response is compassion. When we recognize people who are living with honor and integrity, we feel buoyed in life. And when we can choose to disregard the unjust, we will retain our own peace and ability to respond mindfully—rather than react. The meaning of "disregard" in this context is equanimity—balance or detachment—which is the basis of non-reaction. The idea here is that if we can practice detachment toward those with whom we disagree, we can base our responses in calm awareness, in conscious choice rather than unthinking reactivity. Staying mindful of these choices we have in responding to others—in our smaller community of the classroom and in those larger communities beyond it—can facilitate constructive conversations and interactions within them and thereby help us move toward those futures we hope to create.

This does not mean that we disregard injustice or wrongdoing in the world; on the contrary, it means we respond to them actively yet without clinging to our emotional attachment to a specific outcome. The hope for a specific outcome fuels us. But if we aren't mindful of the primacy of the here and now, of its constant renewal and opportunity, the failure to achieve a specific outcome can debilitate us. Thus, we work in the here and now because the work is essential, and we hope for the future we work to create. But we are mindful of the fact that we are still here and now, not yet there and then. To help me remain mindful of this fact and energized to work in the here and now, I often read Emily Dickinson's brilliant observation:

"Hope" is the thing with feathers—
That perches in the soul—
And sings the tune without the words—
And never stops—at all—.

If we take a literary approach, we can remember the numerous cultural mythologies that suggest "logos"—the word—has the power to manifest reality. Reading Dickinson's poem, we see that which we hope for is as yet wordless, unformed and not yet manifested in the world. Yet we continue the work of signing that world into being, and with mindful awareness, never stop at all.

NOTES

1. Rick Lowe, personal communication, April 21, 2021.
2. I am grateful to the UNF Center for Community-Based Learning for outlining these categories from which I have developed essential questions.

Mindfulness and Movement Practices

*BODY

*Note: Always use extreme caution when beginning or facilitating a new movement practice. Practitioners may be advised to consult a medical professional or trained movement specialist before attempting specific body-based practices. Facilitators should remind practitioners that they must not move in any way that will be injurious or cause pain.

Tree Pose

Tree pose is a primary pose for balance, stability, and grounding. It allows practitioners to find balance and rootedness in the physical body and thereby cultivate emotional and mental balance as well. Balancing postures are best practiced in a well-lit space and with the eyes steady, preferably on a spot toward the floor two or three feet in front of the feet. As practitioners feel more steady and balanced, they can experiment with raising the gaze higher. If one feels the need for added stability and support, move to a wall and allow the hand to touch. (Note: When the right foot is lifted, the left side will be against the wall and vice versa.)

To Practice

1. Standing, feel all four corners of the feet grounded onto the floor. When you're ready, shift the weight into the left foot, imagining rooting down through all four corners of the foot and feeling especially connected through the joint at the base of the big toe. Keep the gaze steady. The hands can be at your sides or on your waist.

2. Feeling strength and activation in your left leg, bring the right foot into contact with the left leg—either propping the right heel against the left ankle or lifting the sole of the right foot onto the left calf or inner thigh. The hands can be used to lift and place the foot, and it's important to keep the foot off the left knee joint.
3. The right knee will be facing right while the left knee and hips face forward. Optionally, you could lift your hands, placing palms together at the heart center or lifting them overhead to "branch out" the tree.
4. Breathe here for three to five breaths before returning the right foot to the floor, feeling steady on two feet, and then switching to the other side.

Community-Building Option

In a group of people, a sense of connection and interdependence can be fostered by turning this practice into a forest of trees. In that case, practitioners will form a circle facing each other. Practitioners will lift their hands to shoulder height with elbows bent, and palms will be placed on the neighbors' hands. Everyone will then practice tree pose, first lifting the right leg into position for several breaths and then the left. Practicing tree pose in a forest demonstrates our dependence on others and how their experiences affect ours. It also promotes teamwork and accommodation of others' needs.

Accommodations

Those who must remain seated should remember that closing the eyes and imagining oneself in a pose activates the same neural pathways in the brain as physically performing the pose, conferring many of the same benefits—particularly mentally and emotionally.

MIND

Five-Senses Meditation

The five-senses meditation is a quick mindfulness exercise in nonjudgmental present moment awareness, bringing practitioners out of the head and into the body. This practice can be used at any time one is feeling the need to center and step outside of a racing monkey mind or emotional confusion. It can also be used as a gratitude practice, cultivating feelings of good will and openness. Facilitators can guide the steps one by one or present the whole practice at the beginning and let practitioners move through the steps at their own pace.

To Practice

1. Silently notice five things you see.
2. Shift your awareness to four things you feel tactilely—the feel of air moving across the skin, the texture of clothing under fingertips, etc.
3. Become aware of three things you hear.
4. Notice two things you smell.
5. Observe one thing you taste—even taking a small sip of a drink or small bite of food to activate this sense.

The steps are easy, rooting practitioners in the here and now. If the steps are practiced quickly enough, there isn't much time for thoughts to wander or judgments about one's observations to creep into the mind.

Accommodations

This can be practiced face-to-face or online, in a classroom or outside, in groups or individually. Those without the functions of hearing or sight can use additional time observing with other senses or can use visualization techniques to imagine what they would see or hear.

SPIRIT

Sharing Light

I encourage this practice to help foster a sense of connection and a spirit of giving. Practitioners can be in a group setting, but the practice can also be engaged when people are alone or remote. It offers a powerful visualization of human interconnection and being of service to others in imagining their greatest good coming to them. In this practice, participants can keep their eyes closed or, if they are in a group of people that has already established some trust, they can pair off and practice while looking each other in the eye—a challenging exercise, because we often have a hard time gazing into each other for extended periods of time. Gazing at each other this way brings a sense of connection and can also bring up many emotional responses in practitioners that have nothing to do with the other person. In such instances, it becomes clear how impactful truly *seeing* each other can be—both on the one seen and on the seer. After such sessions, it is helpful to give practitioners a chance to journal about their experiences, with the option of sharing that reflection with the exercise partner or with the group as a whole.

To Practice

1. Sit in a comfortable, supported position, taking one of the options suggested earlier.
2. Imagine someone else who has a need—this can be someone you know who is sick or suffering, someone you know who needs extra kindness and support, or someone you don't know at all whose needs may or may not be fully known to you.
3. Imagine a thread of light extending from your heart to theirs. On this thread of light, you are sending goodness, love, kindness, vitality, health—any positive quality you hope will be enhanced in their life.
4. With every inhalation, imagine your own heart gaining strength and vitality so that you have ever more to send to the other person while not depleting your own. With every exhalation, imagine the light intensifying and the positive qualities amplifying along the thread, reaching the other person's heart as a suffusing brightness.
5. Continue to inhale and exhale with this visualization pattern for several breaths.

Deepening Option

1. If you feel emotionally strong, you can shift the visualization, imagining on each inhalation that you are receiving the suffering of others in the form of a stream of water entering your own heart. On each exhalation, you can imagine that water flowing down your body, through your legs, and out of your feet into the earth. There, imagine it watering a tree that grows stronger by taking up and transforming it.
2. For either option practiced, after several rounds of visualizing breath, release the visualization and sit for a few breaths with your hands on your heart before releasing the practice.

CONSTRUCTIVE CONVERSATION APPLICATIONS

The exercises described in this section are helpful for cultivating a sense of community, allowing practitioners to observe and even amplify their connection to others. For this reason, practices such as the forest of trees might be helpful early in a group's experience together; practicing together in this way can help with the establishment of trust. It's also a funny exercise, as participants shift and sway due to each other's movements, and laughter serves as a great icebreaker. Guiding a practice of tree pose, on the other hand, might be helpful if a conversation has left participants feeling unsteady emotionally or mentally. Practicing this pose can help participants regain a sense of equilibrium before they move out of the classroom and back into the world. The five-senses meditation is particularly useful when a conversation shifts too far into the hypothetical and participants need to return to the present moment. And the sharing light practice might be used when a group needs to enhance its awareness of interconnection or when people have encountered others' painful stories and don't know how to respond or be of service.

HUMAN BEINGS DOING: MINDFULNESS IN EVERYDAY LIFE

Daily-life applications of the aforementioned practices can be the same as their applications during group conversations. Although we might not ask strangers in a store to form a forest of trees with us, we might find ourselves practicing tree pose before a meeting or phone call we imagine might be challenging. We can use the five-senses meditation when we want to re-root ourselves in the here and now, perhaps when we fearfully follow an imagined narrative in our own heads or when we find ourselves dwelling too long on the past. We can also adopt the sharing light exercise in response to something we see or hear on the news, or we can practice it when we begin to feel at odds with someone closer to us—a coworker or family member, for example. Sending positive thoughts through this practice will certainly help us feel more calmness and compassion; in turn, our more gentle energy is likely to be felt by the other person and may even help them feel more calmness at the moment too.

Chapter 5

The Mindful Classroom
Seeing and Freeing the Whole Student

HOLISTIC TEACHING

Mindfulness encompasses people's personal and interior lives—their mental, emotional, and somatic states of being—in addition to their intellectual production. As such, it offers *holistic* awareness, a word rooted in the Greek term *holos*, meaning "whole." The word holistic was coined in the 1920s in recognition of the fact that nature forms "wholes" that are typically greater than the sum of their parts—a sentiment that mindfulness shares, acknowledging the value of multiple sites of knowing oneself and multiple lenses through which we can view the world.

As I've reflected on ways to teach "whole people," I've been asking myself what exists between thinking and feeling. Where do we locate that space between the two, and what resides there? What do we call it? How do we access it? When there aren't words, there are often images or sounds—we tap into the senses, which are vital avenues for understanding but which are often overlooked in our conventional classrooms. I think this is what artist and educator Lynda Barry means when she discusses the "unthinkable mind," that space between thinking and feeling, between witnessing and imagining. She also writes of "memory without remembering—experiences that don't have to pass through thinking" but are "reformulated by a series of images—written, drawn, sung, sculpted" (Barry 2019, 39). Such memories sound like reflections that are accessed through nontraditional methods and are recalled rather than intellectualized.

In asking students to be reflective, I'm asking them to move into this more holistic—and sometimes soft and vulnerable—space. Because of that, I think it's necessary for them to be aware of what their bodies are feeling as they listen to another, as they tell a story, as they engage in a conversation with like-minded people or a conflict with someone else. I'm interested in helping them access these other, somatic, and sensory sites of information about themselves and their engagement with others.

Mindfulness begins with self-awareness, which is facilitated by reflective practices. Many educators and discussion facilitators have used reflection exercises to help students and other participants lay the groundwork for conversation—helping them first discover their own standpoints, perspectives, beliefs, values, thoughts, and feelings on a topic. Conversely, reflective practices can be used after a conversation or experience, helping participants analyze and integrate new information. From the freewriting exercises of a creative writing classroom to the reflective judgment model of self-assessment, reflection exercises are important tools for engaging students in discovery. When reflection exercises emphasize nonjudgmental present-moment awareness, they cultivate mindfulness. Yet even when the nonjudgmental awareness is brought to bear on past experiences, these exercises can help those who hope to engage in challenging conversations uncover their foundations and determine the next bricks they hope to lay on a path forward.

For example, the "Who Am I? Personal Statement" assignment offered next is one I use at the beginning of many classes that will emphasize race and identity. It allows students an opportunity to reflect on their past experiences, influences, and ideas surrounding who they are and how race has consciously or unconsciously played a part in their identity formation.

Who Am I? Personal Statement Assignment

People have worn race like an invisible badge or a solid burden, like a chip on their shoulders or an albatross around their necks. It's been a mark of shame, a scarlet letter, a source of confusion and blame. For others, it's been carried like a rite of passage, like warrior marks, like an admired or a shameful tattoo. For still more, race has been unquestioned, even unconsidered, like breathing. But race has also been implicated in a question: *what is this really, and how does it shape who I am?*

This question of *Who am I?* is far from unique and in the realm of race studies has provided the basis for countless explorations in sociology, literature, culture, and life. For this assignment, I am asking you to offer a personal definition of race and to consider its role in your individual life. This will be a 750- to 1,000-word reflection on the *personal* meaning of race and racial identity and how this has been shaped by *sociocultural* understandings of race and identity. You are also welcome to write about race in intersectional relationship to other identities you hold.

This reflection can be modeled on Zora Neale Hurston's essay "How It Feels to Be Colored Me." In other words, you can look at the way Hurston constructs her essay to reveal the personal and sociocultural meanings of race in her own life. You can consider the stories Hurston tells, the comments she makes (even subtly) about social responses to race, and how her understanding has been shaped by her life experiences. You can also pay attention to the way she structures her essay and her use of figurative language and other rhetorical devices (such as humor).

You are welcome to use personal anecdotes, and the first-person pronoun is appropriate. You are welcome but not required to use quotations from relevant sources.

Learning Objectives

1. To interpret the meaning(s) of race and identity
2. To describe the function of race in an individual life
3. To evaluate the role of race in one's identity
4. To compare/contrast personal and sociocultural understandings of race

Beyond personally reflective assignments such as this, how else do we help students bring nonjudgmental awareness to their own lives, habits, and histories? How do we help them address the social, political, cultural, environmental, personal, and other types of differences with which they are faced when interacting in diverse communities? Especially in a time of intense change—such as the move from classroom learning to virtual learning in response to COVID-19—many students need additional time for reflection in order to successfully process what is happening and negotiate their responses.

Also, many students appreciate open and honest dialogue about their realities outside of the classroom. Creating space for this starts with groundwork laid when the syllabus is written, from the course description to the contractual arrangement outlined there. When the class first convenes, further groundwork is laid through early discussions on the purpose of the class and the nature of the relationships desired therein. Allowing students an opportunity to help determine the class ground rules and to vocalize their desired outcomes helps them feel ownership for the class and take responsibility for their role in it.

This chapter is dedicated to offering examples of ways in which the classroom itself can be structured as an exercise in and foundation for mindfulness, through conscious decisions about the syllabus, community-based learning projects, assignments, and rubrics—face-to-face and online—and conversations with students.

MINDFUL SYLLABUS

Attentively structuring a classroom as a mindful space begins before the class does. The syllabus, for example, should be honest about the nature of the class. Not only will students engage in traditional academic lessons and assignments, they will also be expected to participate in mindfulness exercises, both in class and on their own. In addition to setting aside at least 10 minutes in each class for mindfulness practices—sometimes at the beginning of class, sometimes at the end, and sometimes both—I've assigned students 10 minutes of mindfulness exercises each day as homework for the duration of our class. In class, I've taught students various practices from which they can choose, but I've also allowed them some freedom in determining their personal mindfulness practices. As long as the practice helps students engage in nonjudgmental awareness of the present moment, then it counts. One student chooses a traditional meditation practice, while another decides that a daily bike ride—undertaken with awareness of her body's sensations, her mental state, and her emotional response—is the best practice for her. Other students may find the "zen" of artistic creation enhances their experiences of mindfulness. Allowing students the liberty of choosing their best personal practice means they will be more likely to commit to it, feel joyfully about it, and reap its benefits—and they will be more likely to maintain these practices after the semester concludes.

To help them remain accountable for the practice, I ask them to log their experiences with mindfulness—including the type of practice, its duration, and their reflections on it:

Meditation Log & Journal

Weekly Journal (add additional blank pages as needed) (table 5.1):

Table 5.1 Meditation Log & Journal.

Day, Date	Type and Duration	Notations on Experience
Sunday		
Monday		
Tuesday		
Wednesday		
Thursday		
Friday		
Saturday		

Credit: Tru Leverette

Typically, I don't collect this information since I want students to remain uncensored and completely honest; however, from time to time in class, I do ask them to volunteer what they are comfortable sharing, and I am always open to their questions about the practices.

Some teachers may feel anxiety about teaching these practices, worrying that their purview is really the academic and intellectual. However, if we hope to teach students as holistic human beings, ones who are resilient in the face of change, and able to experience and find successful outcomes to uncomfortable conversations, then we must help them develop the skills they need in order to do so. The syllabus sets the stage for this holistic awareness, so its tone, structure, and style should convey kindness and understanding of students, recognizing that their most significant lives are lived outside of the classroom. Acknowledging this reality, and connecting with students on this human basis, can help foster a classroom where students feel more comfortable with nontraditional exercises.

A syllabus like this can take a number of forms. I'm fascinated by those whimsical and surreal versions Lynda Barry offers in her book *Syllabus*, and I recommend readers have a look at it to spark their imaginations. As an artist, Barry draws, handwrites, and types the sample syllabi in the book. They contain lots of color and many characters; they are filled with questions and even look a bit chaotic in a way that makes you want to explore them in depth. They're funny and outlandish and clearly convey creativity. Looking at her syllabi, I long to take an art class and let my own creativity manifest. My syllabi, though, have looked more conventional, but I try to convey—in writing and during our first meetings—that our classroom is meant to be a space where students can feel seen and respected as complex individuals.

Sample Syllabus

LITERATURE AND THE EMPATHIC IMAGINATION

Course Description

We can look to literature superficially for entertainment or more deeply for its ability to illuminate life and provide us with windows into diverse experiences. In exposing ourselves to other ways of being in the world, we can spark our empathic imagination, increasing our awareness of and emotional response to realities far different from our own. Our reading in this class will explore transcendental literature and American fiction that we will (hopefully) enjoy, but we will look to texts that allow us to explore the question "How will we be?"

When we consider transcendence in relation to literature, we often think of the transcendental period in the United States of the early 1800s. Believing strongly in the goodness of people and nature, self-reliance and the purity of the individual untainted by social institutions, Transcendentalists saw true community as possible only among individuals who were not corrupted by religious and political institutions. Interestingly, religion itself is used by other individuals as a means through which to gain transcendence—of the body, the material world, the ego, or even the self. This class will take up both threads of the idea of transcendence, exploring transcendental philosophy and then turning to texts of the Yogic tradition. Ultimately, we will explore these philosophies through literary texts in order to consider the nature of transcendence and its purpose and possibilities, both for the self and for the formation of communities.

Our texts will help us delve empathically into others' experiences in order that we question how people in various contexts choose to structure their lives; what is privileged; and what values—both conscious and unconscious—are used to shape lives, relationships, and communities. By extension, our exploration will allow self-reflection on how we want to go about forming our own lives, relationships, and communities.

Course Goals:

1. To foster students' critical thinking, textual analysis, and reasoned argument—both in oral and written forms.
2. To read, reflect upon, and write about American literature.

Course Outcomes—upon completion of this course, students will be able to:

1. Perform literary analysis—both orally and in writing—that demonstrates understanding and use of critical literary theories.
2. Demonstrate critical thinking on historical and contemporary sociocultural and political realities and offer self-reflection on how one chooses to approach these realities.

Texts

The Dude and the Zen Master by Jeff Bridges and Bernie Glassman
   ISBN: 0142180521
Oxherding Tale by Charles Johnson
The Professor's Daughter by Emily Raboteau
The Essential Writings of Ralph Waldo Emerson by Ralph Waldo Emerson
   ISBN: 0679783229

The Portable Thoreau by Henry David Thoreau ISBN: 0143106503
The Yoga Sutras of Patanjali by Swami Satchidananda ISBN: 1938477073
The Bhagavad Gita by Eknath Easwaran ISBN: 1586380192
Song of Myself: The First and Final Editions of the Great American Poem by Walt Whitman ISBN: 1484884493
The Collected Poems of Jean Toomer by Robert B. Jones and Margot Toomer Latimer ISBN: 0807842095

Course Requirements

1. Participation—15%
    You are expected to actively participate in class discussions and to keep track of this participation on the log provided, beginning with week two. As the rubric shows, there are 12 maximum participation points possible each day, equaling 24 points per week, or 312 points for the semester. The week's log will be submitted at the end of each Thursday class.
2. Journal—25%
    You will keep a weekly journal in which you will record your daily meditation practice and as well as life experiences that you find relevant to the issues discussed in the course and our readings.
3. Literary analysis (ten to twelve pages)—30%
    You will write a 10–12 page literary analysis of one of our course texts on a topic you choose in conversation with me.
4. Final Project (maximum 10 pages)—30%
    Your final project will be an autocritography, "an autobiography of a critical concept" (Henry Louis Gates, Jr.), offering critical analysis of a life experience from this semester and its relationship to empathy and/or transcendence.

ASSIGNMENTS

Given the goal of recognizing students as holistic beings, assignments should reflect the diversity of student learning styles. Even in the highly verbal realm of a literature classroom or the precise structure of a math classroom, assignments and outcomes can be reworked to engage students in mindfulness and holistic reflection. For example, visual or graphic submissions (rather than textual ones) might be an option for some assignments. With the increased use of technology, students also have much more ease in creating video projects, podcasts, and other recordings. One art professor has students create artists' journals during a study abroad, resulting in powerful reflections on their learning experience. Even in my literature classrooms, I've used art-based assignments to help students access and communicate nonverbal knowledge.

Sample Art-Based Assignment

Lessons on Love

Our texts this semester deal more with love (and its various manifestations, challenges, requirements, etc.) than with stereotypes of black life. We have read about *Agape* (selfless love), *Philia* (affectionate love, such as that between friends), *Storge* (familial/parental love), and *Eros* (erotic love).

For our next class, read Alice Walker's "Beauty: When the Other Dancer Is the Self" and "Dreaming Ourselves Dark and Deep" and Audre Lorde's "The Uses of the Erotic." You are free to write a standard response paper for these, but you are not required to do so. Instead, I'm asking that you bring in an image you create that represents (all of) our texts' depictions of love. You don't need to limit yourself to these three essays but can address all of the texts we've covered so far this semester. The image you create can be a collage you create of found images, something you draw/paint, or a more metaphorical representation.

The objective here is to think holistically about love, about our texts, about black lives, and to use the more visually creative sides of our brains!

Have fun with this, and be prepared to share your image with the class and to explain your text/image connections.

Authentic assignments are also useful for inviting students' holistic selves into the experience of learning. Authentic assignments are those that ask students to apply what they have learned—often in complex, real-world scenarios. According to Grant Wiggins, such assignments are realistic; expect students to judge and innovate; ask students to "perform," mimic situations that can happen in a workplace or civic life; and allow opportunities for students to practice skills, implement knowledge, and hone their performance of tasks (Wiggins 1998, 22). When such assignments are coupled with reflection, they help students consider their complex responses to work and life situations, fostering their ability to manage difficult experiences when they occur beyond the classroom.

Regardless of what one chooses, holistically aware assignments recognize the diversity of students' learning experiences as well as their interior lives, and tapping into students' ways of knowing beyond the strictly intellectual can yield creative and often richer results.

IN CONVERSATION

If, from the start of the class, the teacher has created a safe place for students to speak candidly, then it will be easier for students to vocalize their experiences of change as the class progresses. Typically, conversations in these classes will not revolve around the handing down of knowledge from teacher to students; instead, students will learn and grow from the processes of listening and voicing. The polyvocality of the conversation is the framework for learning, as students share their stories and try to listen without critique to the stories of others. Usually, the best way to encourage open conversation and student stories is to ask gentle questions, deepening them as the comfort level deepens. Here, I offer examples of such questions for a conversation on race, noting that some or all of these questions could be answered by students in writing before they are asked to volunteer their responses.

Sample Questions for Race-Based Discussion

Opening Questions

1. What is your first remembered awareness of race?
2. What do you know about the history of race/racism in this local community? Nationally? Globally?
3. Often, people have a tendency to think of race relations in terms of black and white. What racism have you seen experienced by other minority groups? Examples can be from the texts we've read or from lived reality.

Deeping Questions

1. How do race relations in the texts we've read mirror race relations in our communities?
2. Where have you experienced or witnessed racism?
3. Where do you see instances of institutional racism—in the texts we've read? In the institutions of which you're a part?
4. How do you think contemporary social justice efforts could be informed by past movements for civil rights?

Reflecting Questions

1. Do you think the steps taken in the books we've read have had positive or negative results in terms of furthering social justice?
2. What concrete social justice actions have you seen that have resulted in tangible, positive change?

3. In order for your life experiences to be more equitable and just, what do you see that needs to change?

A number of these questions are quite personal and could even be painful for participants to think about and address. Educators should remain aware of the individuals in our classrooms: Who are they? How are they feeling? What can we do to facilitate journeys through painful emotions and interactions? There are no easy or quick answers here, but being mindful of the questions is the place where we must begin.

NOTES FROM THE CLASSROOM

The day after the verdict in the Breonna Taylor case was announced, I met virtually with my African Diaspora class. Before class began, one student was visibly upset, and I asked her how she was feeling. She teared up, saying she didn't want to cry but that the verdict was hard to accept. Knowing we had cultivated a virtual classroom of respect and empathy, I asked the students if they wanted to talk about the verdict. Although they didn't jump at the opportunity, I reminded them that we were witnessing in real-time events that are akin to those we had been studying. As we move from the books to the world, we feel very real and valid emotions arising, and we can honor and respect those even in academic spaces. Since students didn't want to talk, I led them in a brief breathing and visualization exercise that, at the very least, helped them feel calmer and more centered. From that place of quiet self-reflection, we began our conversation.

This experience demonstrates empathetic engagement with students as complex human beings. We needn't ask students to check their feelings at the door or to believe they can intellectualize every world event without also acknowledging their emotional responses to those events. When we allow students time to reflect—emotionally and cognitively—we allow them an opportunity to receive broader knowledge, to realize that there are more than just theoretical, intellectual answers to the questions and problems we face.

The breathing exercise I offered was but one opportunity for students to check in with their individual, somatic realities by tuning into their bodies and their physical and emotional state. There are many types of reflections that can help students negotiate such challenges. In moments such as these, stream of consciousness writing, creative writing, and even drawing can offer avenues of reflection. In less stressful moments, casual conversations and daily journals can also provide space for necessary reflection. Part of the mind's eye doesn't think, it sees, especially when one is overrun with emotions. So I've found drawing and doodling to be a useful reflection tool for myself and for students. For many, especially those in a literature classroom, this activity brings them beyond the familiar, helping them tap into creative ways of thinking, imagining, and understanding because they're accessing a different part of the brain. Literature classrooms are highly verbal, but what happens when we tap into the visual? When one class and I discussed intersectionality, I asked them to draw a personal image—perhaps a Venn diagram or other image—that would help them reflect on their multiple identities and locate themselves within this multiplicity. This was a fruitful exercise, and the students visibly enjoyed it. I think it also helped students gain insights they might not have reached had they stayed on the traditionally verbal thought-ways we normally traverse.

Another benefit of reflection is that it can link knowledge with practice and application. According to the Kolb model, there are four stages in an experiential learning cycle. First, students have a concrete experience—they visit a museum, tour a historical site, and so on. This is followed by reflective observation, which involves reviewing and reflecting on the experience: student "re-live" the experience and then evaluate their mental and emotional response to it. Assessing in this way readies them for abstract conceptualization, when students consider what they can conclude from the experience and what they have learned from it. During this phase, students connect their enacted experience with previous knowledge as well as their prior expectations for the experience. The cycle is complete with active experimentation, when students determine the applications of what they have learned, enact their new knowledge, or plan for subsequent learning experiences that build on this one. This final phase allows full integration of the concrete experience, producing authentic learning that bridges knowledge with practice. This cycle illustrates how reflection on an experience allows it to be transformational, helping students assimilate and apply their knowledge. It also shows that the reflective classroom is a mindful one.

The mindfulness exercises that have been detailed in each chapter also show that the mindful classroom is a reflective one. Any of these exercises can be used or modified to help students reflect on their classroom and community-based experiences.

COMMUNITY-BASED LEARNING PROJECTS

Community engagement is one of the best ways to help students integrate and apply their learning, often because such experiences involve reflection, moving their theoretical knowledge to practical application. Since much of what we know is gained through our experiences, I have favored community-based learning experiences for students. According to Strand et al., what is known as community-based transformational learning can take a number of forms for students: community outreach, community-based apprenticeship, community immersion, community-based instruction, or community-based research. Outreach engages students with community members in support of community initiatives; it can take the form of volunteering, philanthropy, or offering community services such as summer camps or health fairs. Apprenticeships immerse students for a specified duration in work settings so that they can practice the skills necessary in those environments. Community immersion is shorter in duration, from a weekend to a semester, such as alternative spring breaks and study abroad experiences. Community-based instruction involves students in service learning, civic engagement projects, and public awareness or education activities. Through these experiences, students deepen their engagement with community groups and the systems in which they are embedded, and students are able to assist the community in fulfilling particular, community-identified needs. Finally, community-based research involves collaboration between researchers and community partners as they engage in discovery and knowledge dissemination. Typically, this research is geared to foster social action and change.

Even during semesters when students don't engage in community dialogue or other forms of outreach or reciprocity, I still take students on site visits relevant to our classroom conversations on race. Living in Northeast Florida, we have the benefit of numerous important historical sites that help students more deeply understand our region's racial history and civil rights efforts. Of course, individual universities will offer guidelines on how to conduct such off-campus visits with students, and typically students are required to sign liability waivers. Nonetheless, site visits offer real-world experiences that activate and help integrate classroom learning. As we know, different people learn best in different ways, so site visits are ways to engage more visual and experiential learners—not to mention, they're usually novel and fun!

Even online classes can call on local students to meet at a specified place and time for a site visit, and most sites—such as museums and state or national parks—offer accommodations for special needs. I've mentioned that during the COVID-19 crisis, one of my classes took a bike tour of a local neighborhood to learn about sites important to black history—following the CDC guidelines for social distancing, small groups (there were only six of us), mask wearing, and being outdoors. This became one of the best site visits I've ever had, not simply because I welcomed being with people again. Our tour guide had a background in urban planning and community development and was able to give us a deep history of this local neighborhood—from its beginnings as a cotton plantation to Harriet Tubman's role there during the civil war to its life during the Jim Crow and post-desegregation eras. We were able to see the land where James Weldon Johnson lived, buildings where

Cab Calloway and Ma Rainey performed, districts that had been industrial or commercial or cultural. Finally, we were able to see firsthand the results of particular zoning policies and botched revitalization efforts. I asked students to reflect on this site visit both prior to and after it was taken, utilizing two sets of questions as a touchstone for their reflections.

Pre–Site Visit Reflection Questions

Before your site visit, take a few moments to free-write on your previous knowledge, your expectations, and your questions regarding the site and/or historical event.

1. What do you know or what have you heard about the site or event?
2. What are your expectations regarding your visit? (Consider, for example, how you might feel there, what you might need to experience the visit fully, other similar experiences you have had, etc.)
3. What questions do you have about the site/event? What do you want to know?

Post–Site Visit Reflection Questions

Take a moment to review the free-write on expectations/questions you produced before our site visit. Then, considering your experience at the visit, write a reflection that answers the following questions.

1. What did you learn? (What was new, surprising, noteworthy?)
2. What connections can you make between our classroom/textual knowledge and the real-world knowledge gained through the site visit?
3. Were your initial questions answered? If so, what were the answers?
4. What do you still want to know?

Student reflections can be in direct response to these questions, or the questions can merely be guides to help students begin processing the experience. And the form student responses take can vary as well—textual or visual, digital or low-tech. The form is open, allowing students to be creative and mindful of their individual ways of processing information and, thus, allowing a multiplicity of deliverables to emerge.

Even if in-person experiences are restricted or otherwise not possible, there are many virtual avenues that can mimic a site visit. Many museums offer virtual tours, allowing students to visit extensive collections without leaving home. Additionally, being open-ended about some of the site visits can be helpful, as it will allow students to find physical resources in keeping with their individual research agendas. One student visited a different neighborhood with an important role in black history, while yet another used her volunteering with a local nonprofit to connect her with vital historical information and interview sources.

Below is an example research assignment and community-based learning project that I developed for a class on the African Diaspora that also explored our region's local African American history. This assignment is flexible enough to be useful for face-to-face or virtual classes, and although it's locally relevant, it could be tailored for other topics and regions.

Diaspora Research Assignment and CBL Project

This assignment is designed to meet a number of student learning objectives. In particular, it is geared toward the CBL outcomes that ask students to

- locate and analyze contributions of various African cultures to the mainstream culture of local and global diasporic communities and
- relate the connections between theoretical, text-based knowledge and "real-world" applications/manifestations of this knowledge.

This umbrella assignment includes your research assignment and community-based learning project. As such, it has a number of components:

- Statement of interest
- Final essay
- Bibliography
- 20/20 Voices contribution
- DHI Showcase poster/presentation

Instructions

Considering the diaspora within Florida generally or Northeast Florida specifically, find a topic of interest to you. For example, you might want to research one of the following:[1]

- Mary McLeod Bethune
- James Weldon Johnson
- Zora Neale Hurston
- Clara and Eartha White
- The Florida Black Heritage Trail
- Civil Rights in Jacksonville, Ax Handle Saturday

- Civil Rights in St. Augustine, St. Augustine Four
- American Beach, Manhattan Beach
- Fort Mosé
- Norman Studios
- Florida's Black Cowboys (recently, there was a traveling art exhibit on Florida's black cowboys sponsored by the Florida Agricultural Museum)
- Consolidation
- Contemporary anti-racism activism locally
- Contemporary art/ists locally (6 Ft. Away Gallery, Yellow House, Erin Kendrick, etc.)

Also, you may explore the following resources for topics of interest:

Images of Florida's Black History
Florida's Black History
Florida Black Heritage Trail
Ten Stops Along Florida's Black Heritage Trail
St. Augustine's Black Heritage
Plantation Slavery in Antebellum Florida
Black Demographics Florida
Reverse Migration
Rosewood Massacre
ACCORD Civil Rights Museum/ACCORD Freedom Trail
Lincolnville Museum and Cultural Center
Norman Studios
Rhoda L Martin Cultural Heritage Center

Do not limit your search to these suggestions, but feel free to use them as a starting point for further investigation. Once you have narrowed a topic of interest, begin your research to explore the topic in more detail, taking careful notes and documenting your sources for your bibliography.

You will provide me with a STATEMENT OF INTEREST[2] on [date]. This statement should be no more than three pages and should state your topic of interest and your rationale for wanting to research it. This rationale should include

- A brief summary/history of the topic
- A personal statement of why this topic is of interest to you
- A brief consideration of why this topic is significant to diaspora studies locally
- A note on any relevant site that could be visited, including the address, contact information and, if applicable, a web address
- A bibliography of research to date

Subsequently, you will work outside of class, researching, *safely visiting relevant sites*,[3] writing your pre– and post–site visit reflections, and writing an essay on the topic. On [date], you will be responsible for submitting to me an eight- to ten-page *ESSAY* that includes

- A history of this topic
- A summary of any site visit and impressions
- An analysis of why this topic is significant to the diaspora in Florida and/or in Jacksonville, both historically and contemporarily
- A discussion of how this information could be used to forward anti-racism (activism, education, community connections, suggestions for future application, etc.)
- A bibliography of research, including appropriate citing of the sites visited

I plan to provide my feedback on your essays on [date]. You will need to revise your essay based upon my feedback by [date], and will then record your essay (either in part or in full) for the *20/20 VOICES* podcast (aaads.domains.unf.edu/voices).[4]

Digital Humanities Institute Showcase

We are also planning to participate in the DHI Showcase through virtual poster presentations.

See information from the DHI director below:

The annual Digital Projects showcase will be held remotely during the week of [date], with several events scheduled synchronously for [date].

The call for proposals is now open. All members of the university community are invited to participate, and we also invite proposals from individuals or groups representing other universities or cultural institutions. We are interested in presentations dealing with projects at any stage of development, as well as presentations on methods and tools. Presentations may highlight a project in its entirety or may address a specific aspect of a larger undertaking. Proposals are due [date], with acceptance notification by [date].

Proposal submissions should include the following: (1) full title of poster/presentation; (2) names of all participants, with academic/professional title (or major/program of study for students); (3) a description/abstract of the material to be presented (250 words max.); (4) name of faculty mentor or project leader, if applicable, and an explanation of any special needs regarding technology or equipment.

Students have connected deeply with our local history and community in tackling this assignment, and they are proud to see products of their work made public. Our 20/20 Voices podcast broadcasts their voices into the larger community, allowing students to teach others these important and often overlooked histories, to tell the untold stories. Their poster presentations have been visually engaging and intellectually stimulating, and they too allow students' work to reach a wider audience.

Following is a Poster One Student Created for this Assignment

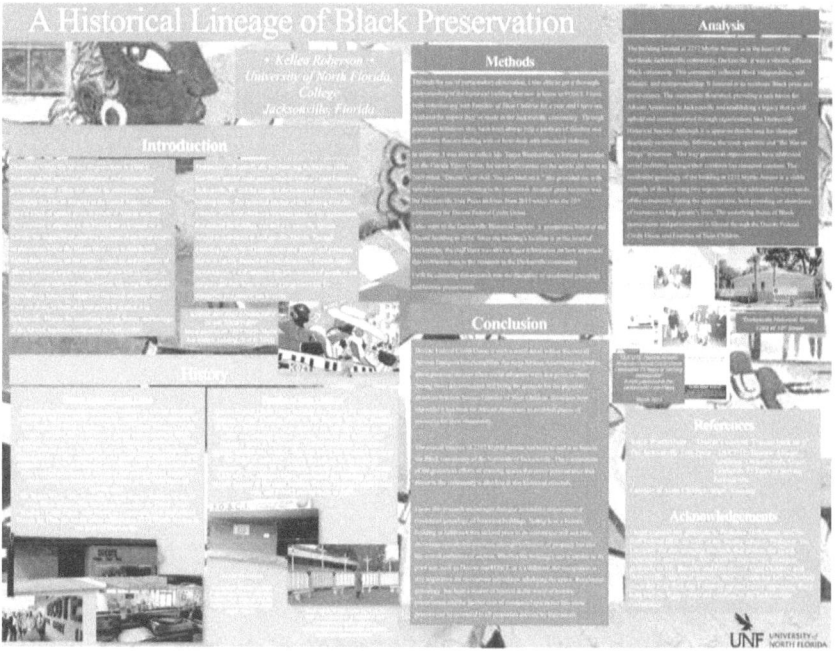

Figure 5.1   *Source*: Kellea Roberson.

In *Teaching Community*, bell hooks writes, "Classroom settings can be a place where we all learn the practice of freedom" (hooks 2003, 21). We practice the freedom of existing holistically in a mindful classroom, where the realities of students and teacher outside the classroom are not only acknowledged but also mined as a source of knowledge. We practice freedom in sharing our stories, in recognizing our spirits as well as our minds, in deciding consciously how we will be. The mindful classroom is a powerful place because it practices and enlivens these freedoms. It is life happening, unique and individual selves developing and being and being in community with others. It is imperfect and organic, hopeful and evolving—as are we.

NOTES

1. Note that there are resources on some of these topics in our online course files.

2. You will use this statement of interest as the basis for your poster proposal for the DHI Showcase. The poster presentation can be a collaborative project, meaning you are free to join forces with classmates working on congruent topics and prepare together a poster presentation. Proposal information and due date can be found below.

3. Ideally, we will visit sites as a group. However, given unique restrictions and precautions due to COVID-19, we may not be able to undertake group site visits. I will do my best to arrange them, but they may not be possible this semester.

4. Additionally, I have been thinking about working with students on what I'm calling the "Subversive Memory Book of North Florida History" and would like to consider using the essays from this class in the book.

Chapter 6

Student Voices
Reflections from Mindfully Engaged Students

NOT SUCH A BLACK-AND-WHITE ISSUE: RACE IN AMERICA

by Matthew Welcome

My identity has been caught in a perpetual war of worlds, and it is a miracle that each branch of society that wishes to claim me has not torn my brown, battered vessel totally asunder. I come from white; I come from black. I love white; I love black. I am perpetually embarrassed by white; I resent black. I appear brown, yet neither side wishes to acknowledge a sizeable connecting line between white and black, a bridge of brown bodies, so to say, and I, alongside many other mixed people, am trapped in the middle. My life exists somewhere in the nebulous chasm between races, a chasm that is too complicated for anyone to willingly want to ford. I am simultaneously craved and rejected by both sides; I am far too black to be white, but I am far too white to be black. And so I exist between races, the bastard child of two warring civilizations, too complicated to be understood by either. The idea of race complicates me; by its existence, I turn the black-and-white problem of race in America into a black-and-white-and-brown problem, and the mystery of how to solve it all becomes continually harder to navigate.

I understand society's conundrum; if more variables are introduced to a supposedly dichotomous problem that has gone unsolved for hundreds of years in America, we may never see through to the end of it. However, society's unwillingness to expand the conversation far past a racial dualism does not make the struggles I face as a result of my unique position any less pertinent; it is through this unique position that I become a problem. In an issue that has been presented as black-and-white in America's contemporary racial climate, I am perpetually pitted against myself. One arm always seems to apply the shackles that another arm is required to break. To echo the sentiments of W. E. B. Du Bois, I ever feel my fourness—an American, a Negro, multiracial, white; four souls, each clamoring for sovereignty in a body that wishes to achieve equilibrium. I do not believe that these identities must be severed to thrive; I believe that they are already so deeply entangled and entrenched in each other's histories that they need to do no more than open their stubborn eyes to see and appreciate our similarities and differences. This Pollyanna-like wish for equilibrium is, I believe, a glint of hope found in the eyes of any American who has not given up on the hope that racial relations in America could improve. As racial relations improve, as the social thunderstorm of race relations starts to calm, so does the war of worlds inside my brain. Until America hits this equilibrium, however, the ideological battlefield of my brain remains a wreck, a farrago of mismatched pieces in a bewildering puzzle.

According to the races I possess, I am a walking paradox. Every trait within me is made oxymoronic by their corresponding trait within the opposite race. I am a poor and rich, a victim and an oppressor, uneducated and brilliant, dignified and unbecoming. These traits clash with each other in my head, but I do not surmise that any of them have to do with my race. For the most part, many of these traits are projections, stereotypes of the larger groups I fit into that have been unfairly thrust upon me due to the color of my skin and the cultures that accompany them. Listening to rappers like MF Doom, YBN Cordae, and Kendrick Lamar and aspiring to attend an Ivy League graduate school are not mutually exclusive ideas, but society sees rap (a socially black idea) and intelligence (a socially white idea) as irreconcilable. Society at large sees black culture and shakes its head, dismissing it as uneducated, excessively materialistic, and filled with unsavory vices. Society sees white culture as excessively bland, ignorant, derivative, and occasionally nonexistent. Yet here I am, a microcosm of certain aspects of both of my inherited cultures, and I do not suffer because of it. I often find myself at the crossroads of these cultures, picking and choosing the fruits I see in each land's garden rather than the weeds and creating for myself an intercultural Garden of Eden. I feel as if this is the ideal that racial relations have to offer; each society has different experiences, traits, ideas, luxuries, and goods to offer each other, and the closer we get to racial equilibrium, the closer the Garden gets to becoming a cultural plaza that each society can acknowledge the goodness in and learn from.

I harbor an odd sentimentality toward progress in racial relations in American history, because I feel as if each warring race within me has an opportunity to feel pride with each step forward. When I learned about the passing of the Civil Rights Act of 1964, my black portion leapt for joy, for my white side had never known oppression due to race. When I learned about the result of *Brown v. Board of Education*, I leapt for joy, for I felt as if each side of me reconciled, if only for a moment, and all felt as if it were at peace. As I learned of the passing of *Loving v. Virginia*, I felt truly whole, because each half of my existence was fully validated by the country I call home. I see glimmers of peace in these steps forward, and the inspiring aspect of these steps is that many of them have taken place in the last two centuries. If we continue the frequency with which we walk toward this goal of true racial equity, or if we increase the rate, we can dramatically improve the race relations in this country to a level we couldn't have conceived before the civil rights movement. This hope is no pipe dream; it is potential. If my enslaved forefathers could see the progress we have made up until this point, I believe they would be proud of how far we've come. I also believe they would acknowledge that black citizenship and American citizenship are still fundamentally different terms, and they would know that we still have much progress to go.

My hope does not blind me from reality; my hope is a response to reality. My hope is the product of progress and my natural response to revolution. To quote James Baldwin, "I live a hope despite my knowing better." To keel over and accept that the world is cruel and unchanging is unfair and unproductive to the strides American society has made. Despite this, we still have a long way to go, and my hope prompts me to fight, tooth and nail, to do my part until society starts heading down that path of progress; from this path, we came and to this path we will hopefully return until we have righted everything we can right in society. My whiteness hopes in my darkness and my darkness hopes for my whiteness. As I naturally assume the position of a mediator between the races, a bridge connected by the point at which my warring colors meet, I will do my best to ensure the prosperity of all races. No race is any less American than the other, and all races should be able to criticize America's racial shortcomings because we believe in a country that can always do better. It is here in this Whitman-esque universality that I hope, on behalf of our nation, that we can all press toward a love that acknowledges the beauty and importance of all races and cultures without having to trample on another. I am grateful for the cultures I have inherited, and their intersection highlights the balanced peace that disparate races can undoubtedly find.

Race can assume the form of the chains that bind, or it can act as the wild dance of freedom from bondage, and its function lies in both the hands of the individual and the society as a whole. The followers of Baby Suggs's teachings in *Beloved* loved themselves and their skin despite the white people who didn't. However, a society that believed in race as binding chains quashed their love and their spirits, and they were unable to experience freedom in their own skins. When, as a society, we can begin to appreciate people without skin color as a caveat, we too can dance the dances of freedom, happy to be in our own skin(s). It is not enough for one society to prosper at the detriment of another; we must all break the idea of race as a binding chain together to achieve a national equilibrium, a true "land of the free." To finally achieve this "land of the free," however, will undoubtedly require the collective efforts of a galvanized, passionate "home of the brave."

CREPUSCULAR

by sierra jones-frishman

crepuscular: resembling twilight—dim—indistinct
You see, my corned beef is riddled with cloves and peppercorns, and hauled out of a huge pot. It is dressed with spicy-brown mustard on a plate with boiled cabbage and ketchup on the side. My corned beef is also seared with fresh onions and scotch bonnet, and spooned out of a pan, by way of a can. It is adorned with pickapeppa on a plate with stir-fried cabbage and rice on the side. Each platter holds a special place in my grandmothers' repertoires. But one shimmies to popular Motown and watches Westerns, and the other sways to roots Reggae and watches *Passa Passa* plays.

You see, there is also plenty plantain in my life. My *banan peze* come fried, then smashed, and then fried again. They are eaten straight out of the cast iron pan, covered with *pikliz*. My *pasteles* come stuffed with *pollo*, then wrapped with banana leaves, and then secured with twine. They are eaten with the same amount of patience as it takes to make them. Each platter is an extension of my step-grandmothers' grace. But one used to shake her hips to Sweet Mickey's Kompa, and the other still glides to Hector Lavoe's Salsa.

It took me too long to stop explaining how and why i listen to The Black Keys and to Eric B. and Rakim; how and why i say "pear" instead of "avocado"; how and why i can sing "*Sak pasé!*" to the *boulanje* attendant before i order more *pate ayisyen* than i can eat; how and why i can laugh while eaves-dropping on the *bochinche* of Nuyorican women in line at the bodega but am too afraid to join in. There was never, is never, enough time to interpret. There was never, is never, an end to the translations. Crepuscular-me devoured the faces brightened by the possibilities of me, only to later be darkened by disappointment.

~ ~ ~

i could have an orgy with all of the sierras i've been mistaken to be. Some new, some old, yet all as equally fictitious as they are faulty. i have been, and will be: the beckoning, biracial beauty; the coy, Caribbean *coolie*; the down-to-fuck foreign; the giggling, jiggling jezebel; the lil' alluring light-skinned. i have rarely been noticed as a conscious kween from Queens; a new-school, neck-rolling, New York City nerd; a pessimistic poet plotting on the revolution; a seriously stoic sister; a witty, working, womxn full of wanderlust. Crepuscular-me studied the faces twinkling and shape shifting at the sight of me, all the while obscuring "the light" within. i cooed nights away while the twilight in my life flickered quietly.

My Jamaican mother once stood on a sidewalk to surprise me when i was 12. She waited for me to emerge from the gleaming glass doors of Trinity School, the number one private school in the country, according to Forbes that year. My elation to share the subway ride home with my mother, while we gossiped over a plate of stew peas, was soon taken. The nosey Manhattan mothers could not place her, so they mistook her for my nanny.

i once went to pick up my Haitian-Jamaican brother Malcolm from kindergarten when i was 14. The nosey Queens mothers could not place me. So they sent the one with the heaviest Caribbean accent over to say, "Your son is so cute."

i once went to watch my Puerto-Rican brother Christopher play in a little league game when i was 16. The nosey Long Island mothers could not place me. So they sent the blondest one over to spit, "Who do you belong to?"

i once went to take my Haitian-Jamaican sister Sabrina Joy to the club to dance our pains away when i was 22. The nosey Jacksonville women could not place me. So they sent the most masc.-presenting one over to ask, "Who you here wit?" She slurred there was no way we were sisters because i was light-skinned and therefore more lovely.

i once went to pick up my white-passing brother Jonah from a friend's birthday party when i was 23. The nosey Long Island mothers, and lascivious husbands, could not place me. So they sent the tannest one over to sigh, "You must be (insert only-Black-child-at-the-party's name here)'s sister." When i insisted i was Jonah's sister, she laughed a "For real?"

~ ~ ~

You see, i have learned to wear my Blackness as a shield in front of the white fragility i have inherited. i also hold it as a firm guard against the other sierras i am not. Crepuscular-me practiced burying "the light" deep within me, where the estimations and calculations of others could not reach.

i once tossed over a beer pong table at a dorm party because its white players ignored my demands to stop singing "nigga" along to Kendrick Lamar's "M.A.A.D City" when i was 19. A large white boy yelled through me, "Someone come get this black bitch." i offered to kick his ass like the man he alleged he was. He grabbed me by the neck in response. It was not my white "sisters" who tried to stop that white boy. It was my black siblings who pried him off while i beat his face in. This was the first time i was called a "Black bitch" and i was proud.

i once told my white father that a white boy grabbed me by the neck, after i told him not to call me a Black bitch, when i was 20. My father scolded me for becoming violent, reminding me of my sex. i asked him if i should have shouted, "Wait! My father's white!" instead. My father—who introduced me to The Pharcyde and gave me my first mixed Hip-Hop CD; who knows all the words to KRS-One's "Sound of da Police"; whose children have mothers of color—cried when i reminded him i am a black person.

~ ~ ~

twilight: diffused light from the sky when the sun is below the horizon—terminal period after full development—vagueness or gloom

You see, my callings and sufferings, vocations and valedictions have not led me to twilight's delicate torment. It is the realization that what is more strenuous than running away is simply standing still. Twilight-me grovels in the ills, embraces the purposeful evasion of others, and licks the crimson cuts of curiosity in order to replenish the iron-will of accountability.

You see, my mind has moved me toward *Disintegration*, *Invisible Man*, and *Their Eyes Were Watching God*. My studies have driven me through *The Fire This Time*, *The New Jim Crow*, and *Toward Psychologies of Liberation*. My spirit has sipped on *Helium*, baby's *Islandborn*, and *Peluda*. There is comfort in consciousness collected, memory in marked marvel, and pressure in the provoking of words.

What do i gather, then, about this place where i hunt for home when held most dear are *Ain't I a Woman*, *Beloved*, *Black Boy*, *Black Marxism*, *Black Power*, *Black Unicorn*, *The Body Keeps the Score*, *Sister Outsider*? Stories of alienation, bruising from beating, demons, healing, longing, salvation, and worthwhile-yet-weary work are embedded in my shoulder brushing hoops.

The cover of twilight's shadows is a gift of all the secrets my ancestors whispered to the moon. It's a machete hidden in the front closet for intruding masterminds. It's a broom behind the front door against the drifting dead, set on disturbing our homes. It's a pussy pink tongue picking apart the operative opinions of those whose oppressed minds play tricks on them.

i once saw a sign on I-95 promoting its "Interactive Jungle Room" when i was 24. The sign professed one could find "the weirdest stuff in St. Augustine" next to a little white child holding an ivory African mask. My stomach told more about my body's brooding than my laughing face did.

i once attended a si-star circle of healing on a clear Taurus full moon when i was 24. i wandered barefoot around the B&Sun Arts and Culture Center and gazed upon the vintage baskets, furniture, paintings, and sculptures so bountifully black, so unapologetically African. Upon rounding the fourth corner, i fretted as the faces of the black womxn i've fallen in love with in my studies were missing. i circled the vintage photographs once more so i could reciprocate blessings before them. i believed *i'd* not taken care. But it was not me who'd made haste, mistook, or overlooked, it was my brothers who'd forgotten. My heart reached out further than my mind could carry beyond the loss i embodied when i found no Brooks, nor Davis, nor hooks nor Lorde nor Shakur among the exalted.

i once read a book titled *The Birth of African-American Culture*, when i was 24. When i search on Google the names of the 1970s authors, i saw white faces staring back. My silent shake of my head and little else told more than a furious fire would.

i once addressed a class lacking in faces of color about negligence and stereotypes in the media when i was 24. "A shooting in Moncrief is not news because there are shootings there all the time. If it happened at Jacksonville Beaches or UNF that would be another story," a classmate claimed. When i addressed him, his ignorance and his lack of consideration, my professor said to me "Now, you don't have to get upset." A white woman in the class, unprompted, later asked me at a club meeting why i was so defensive in class. When i sarcastically responded "Apparently a Black womxn saying holding the lives of white people over Black people in the news is ignorant is being defensive," she resigned from the group.

Twilight-me adorns my doubts in cowrie shells and dreams of great-grandmother Olive when i'm between riches. Twilight-me sweetly caresses the fragility i find before offering it up to Erzulie Dantor. Twilight-me chooses to uphold the world's demand that i grip onto my genius with Isis's might. Most importantly, twilight-me calls on others to summon theirs; we have no choice to be citizens of this world as the position is inalienable. Any cynicism creates a cover for excusing. Any denial is a directive of the doomed.

Twilight-me bellows in my Blackness by ancestry, by blood and by history. My Blackness is righteously undefined, gorgeous in its grief. Its glitter, into darkness, foretells my resilience, my resurgence and my resistance. In twilight's shroud, i am free.

WHO AM I? A SECOND LOOK

by Michael Coutu

"I am most interested in blackness at its borders, where it meets whiteness, in fear and hope, in anguish and love, just as I am most drawn to the line between self and other, in family, friendship, romance, and other intimate relationships." (Emily Bernard, *Black is the Body*)

Most discussions of race in America are doomed to failure from the moment they begin. This is because the participants both imagine race as something which is defined and agreed upon, as though it were no more slippery than "concrete." Almost any reasonable person, if asked, would respond that all humans belong to a single race. While they may think this is what they believe, the reality of their actions reveals that there is some subtle disconnect between their mind and body. The failure lies in the difference between their definition of the word and their conceptualization of it. Defined by a society, race may be some agreed upon tool of taxonomy, creating castes and classes as a result of social contract. Defined instead by the individual, race is a muddied concoction; a bathtub brew of class, culture, ethnicity, and racial stereotypes. The fact that I did not begin to construct my own personal definition of race based on skin color is a testament to my privilege. My complexion is a light tan, light enough that I was ushered forward without resistance, past the age where society appraises new arrivals as White or Other, and into the age where I began make my own assessments. It would be many years before I would begin to feel that my classification did not match my experience, as though I have been admitted into an exclusive club by error, and that at any moment I will feel a tap on my shoulder, followed by a voice saying something like "Sorry, *Sir*, but there appears to have been a mix up. May I see your ticket, please?"

The first house I remember living in was just a block away from my grandparents' home. I spent most of my early childhood not in my own house, but in theirs. My parents weren't abusive or negligent, but they were very poor, and I'm grateful I didn't have to spend much time thinking about it. My father drove down city streets early each morning, rummaging through trash cans and dumpsters for anything he thought he could sell. Then he was gone entirely. My mother was already working overtime, and so my younger sister and I would stay with my grandparents from early each morning until after dinner, every day. They are Cuban immigrants who assimilated into their new home and embraced all aspects of it, including the language. Growing up, my grandparents spoke English in the house, as did my mother, and so neither my sister nor I speak Spanish. For us, bonding with others who share our ethnic background often comes to an abrupt and absolute halt once this language barrier is revealed. Within the community, someone who doesn't speak Spanish isn't Latinx, they are White. Another tap on my shoulder, another voice informing me my membership has been revoked.

As I grew older, I began to witness class discrimination and added more to my definition of race. I was nine years old when we were evicted from that childhood home near my grandparents. My oldest sister had divorced her husband and was living with her two children in a low-income housing project on the other side of town. My mother applied, and after a week living with my grandparents, we were accepted and moved in. My mother was devastated, but I couldn't have been happier. My niece and nephew are only two years younger than me, and we were already very close. There was a playground, and lots of other kids, and the complex down the road had a fence around the swimming pool that you could slip right through when no one was looking. I grew close with the families of my new friends, went to parties in their homes, and cared for their younger siblings while their parents worked. I ate lumpia and honey drippers and mangoes with chile and lime; I drank powdered milk and waited in line with my friends during summers for free lunch.

We lived in that apartment for three years, and I felt at home until the day I left. The realities of moving aren't lost on teenagers, and my friends and I knew we were saying goodbye for good. They were genuinely happy for me, joking around while loading boxes, but I remember one of them saying that we'd probably earned a record for living there longer than any other white family. My niece and nephew are much darker than I am, their skin is the color of coffee with cream, even though their mom is lighter than I am. When I heard them laughing, it shocked me. I laughed it off, because I didn't know why it hurt me so much to be called "White." I'd met White people before, met both of their parents at the same time, been in their homes for dinner and found out what they ate; I didn't know what I was, but I knew a few things I was not. I didn't know what to say. I just knew that I'd never felt like I didn't belong while I lived there, and that none of the White families I'd ever met would have said the same. Yet I had learned from their laughter and the laughter of my friends that I had always been an outsider.

Since race is not the color of our skin, or our families, or the countries our families came to America from, or the poverty or wealth which we have experienced, what is left? Eliminating what race isn't brings us closer to understanding that what makes people different has nothing to do with what makes people human. The goal then becomes to align ourselves on our shared humanity, to reduce the stigma that comes with our "otherness." We have hurt our fellow humans for hundreds of years, all the while using race as the definitive standard for exclusivity. Given the depths of the damage it causes, race will take time to relinquish its hold on America. By encouraging others to share their experiences, listening without judgment, and sharing our own experiences without shame, we can begin to truly bear witness to our shared humanity. By searching always for the borders along our stories, we can carry America forward into a land of inclusiveness, unity, and purpose only it can achieve.

REFLECTION

by Kellea Roberson

As my college career comes to an end, I have begun to worry that I am not prepared for the "real world," my future job or graduate program. I have always been an overthinker, trying to process different scenarios and outcomes in order to make an informed decision, but then returning to the decision-making process for a total of fourteen times or more. However, I never thought twice about receiving a minor in African American/African Diaspora studies, and thankfully I did not. I believe the time I spent in this minor has accounted for more than half of the knowledge I have attained from the university. This minor has provided me with the necessary knowledge to understand my own history and heritage, making up for the information I was not taught in school. I will forever be grateful for the professors that taught these classes. I have had the opportunity to take two classes with Dr. Tru, "Black American Literature" and "African Diaspora." In these discussion-based courses, I have been able to challenge my own ideas of race, nationality, citizenship, the diaspora, and identity. It has been an eye-opening experience that has guided my understandings of these topics and is truly a privilege that I do not take lightly. Upon entering African Diaspora, I wanted to be exposed to the diaspora outside of the United States. Throughout my own knowledge of the diaspora, the focus is North American centered, but in actuality, there are more people of African descendant in Brazil than the States!

I do recognize that in this short period of time, we would not be able to explore all—or even half—of the full diaspora. However, through the textbooks, specifically, *The African Diaspora: A History through Culture* by Patrick Manning, I was able to find an extensive list of literature, articles, and resources to expand my knowledge of the diaspora. In addition, I appreciate the approach we took when examining the diaspora, not understanding it through race, the color of one's skin, but also mapping it through culture, language, and the actual movement of bodies. I never realized how the hyper focus of race can limit the understanding of the diaspora until taking this course. That is not to say that I do not think race is pertinent, but rather one part of studying the diaspora and should be observed with the understanding that race was created through colonial lenses. In class, we discussed the faults of some literature and scholars in diaspora research, mainly the way it has been romanticized and homogenized by scholars in the United States. In some ways, it is rather nice that African Americans, in particular, are able to have this "black Utopia" known as "Africa," but it is very damaging in the way it portrays African cultures and the overall essence of the continent and countries within it. I was scrolling through social media and seeing how

African Americans, me included, tend to view Africa as the motherland where we will eventually return, but were to exactly? I asked my father about "the Motherland" and he responded, "You mean Louisiana?" He told me that we can barely trace our roots to slavery in the United States, so what makes me think I can trace it back through the Atlantic Slave Trade to the village or tribe we originated from. I used to get upset with him about it, but then I realized me wishing for this "black Utopia" called "Africa" is not recognizing the beautifully crafted history of my ancestors in the United States.

This class has also helped in beginning my quest in mindfulness, in the way I think, react, and respond. At the start of this class, Professor Tru had us read *Taming the Ox* by Charles Johnson. When I first opened the book, I was confused so I researched the author to get a better understanding of the text. I found the book to be valuable; throughout the first month of the term I kept referring back to Johnson's chapters; being able to view the "Other" with the absence of my own assumptions and judgment is something that I have been working on diligently. The work is hard, but it is clarifying to view people outside of my own judgments and understand that everyone has their reasons for being where they are and who am I to pass judgment on them? In addition, I have incorporated 10 to 15 minutes of mindfulness mediation to my day. Sometimes I can't focus because my mind is racing but I remember in class Professor Tru explained there are many, many, and many forms of mindfulness meditation, and there is no right or wrong way to foster a mindset that is peaceful and full of non-judgment. I am glad that I took this course at the time that I did; this semester I was worried about my peace, my health, and my academics. This class helped me refocus and maintain a positive mindset amid a chaotic world.

REFLECTION

by Deqa Moussa

I originally enrolled in this class because it was listed as a Lit course and I needed it for graduation. Though unintentional, this class has become my favorite course I have ever taken. Our field trips outside the classroom into the real world changed my perspective of Florida. When I first moved here, I thought Jacksonville was just another white town in the south. I never knew the rich cultural history of the city or the fact that Northeast Florida was such an important place during the civil rights movement. I will never forget our trip to American Beach where Amber, Theo, and I had the opportunity to talk to Ms. Nelly who lived right on the beach. Learning about the community from the community is the only way to do it. Something Rodney

Hurst said stuck with me: you cannot teach me my history. I'm paraphrasing but I really took it to heart; I cannot truly learn about someone's history and struggles unless I can get their firsthand experience and I surely cannot teach it to them. I went for a walk around St. Augustine and came across a plaque that stated Martin Luther King, Jr. was here. I am ashamed to say that I had no idea he came to St. Augustine at all. Another thing that shocked me was my ignorance about the diaspora. It never occurred to me that Africans were traveling across the world prior to the slave trade. This seems silly in retrospect because my family comes from Somalia and I grew up with the knowledge that we were nomadic people who traveled by horse, camel, and boat. Learning that East Africans were a part of Indian nobility was probably one of my favorite things.

Conclusion

Where Are We Going? Communities to Come

LOVE LIKE THAT

A few years ago, I was asked to give a talk at the main branch of our city's public library. In considering the library's proposed title for the talk, "What We Do for Love," I thought of that old song: "The Things We Do for Love." And humming that song, I thought: we do everything that challenges us.

We take care of our children when they are sick.
We call our friends when they are lonely.
We make the grand gestures of romantic getaways with our significant other.
And we offer the small acts of taking out the garbage and doing the dishes.

And then I thought of Tina Turner asking "What's Love Got to Do with It?" In answer to that, I thought: it's got to do with everything worthwhile. And then of course I asked *why?*, which has had me contemplating love ever since.

First, I pondered definitions, and I'd like you to consider what you think about when you hear the word "love." Perhaps the face of someone close to you: a spouse or child, a parent or close friend, even a pet. We're accustomed to thinking of hearts, cupids, and Valentine's Day roses, but none of these images, these things, truly points to love itself. Let's think for a moment, then, about what love is, and, since I teach literature, let's turn to some literary minds for inspiration:

- George Sand tells us, "There is only one happiness in this life, to love and be loved."

- Oscar Wilde urges us, "Keep love in your heart. A life without it is like a sunless garden when the flowers are dead."
- With Frank Sinatra, love becomes a joke: "Alcohol may be man's worst enemy, but the bible says love your enemy."
- And Rumi says, "Let the beauty of what you love be what you do."

As much as I'm a fan of Rumi, I have to ask: What does that even mean, with all those abstractions?!

It's those abstractions that muddle us on the issue of love. Joyce Carol Oates is onto something more concrete when she writes: "In love there are two things—bodies and words." The reason love is so hard to define is because we so often confuse feeling (or words) for action (or what we do). In reality, love isn't a feeling at all (and this isn't a new idea), although certain sentiments such as compassion or passion, camaraderie or intimacy can lead to the actions of love. My mother used to tell me that *feelings* matter most to those who are feeling them. In other words, you can never be sure of the way I feel when I tell you my feelings. I can tell you I love you, but what does that mean to you? Does it make you feel the exact way I feel? How can we be sure? You can only be sure of the way I feel when I show you my feelings by what I do. I can tell you I love you, but more importantly I must show you. Shakespeare says it best, then: "They do not love that do not show their love."

My library talk was originally titled "What We Do for Love," but I think we might more productively talk about "What We Do AS Love." In order to do that, I want to talk about two things that are closely linked and might even be the essence of love. The first is service. The second is growth.

SERVICE

Recently, I published an essay in which I wrote about love as service.[1] The essay looks at Charles Johnson's novel *Oxherding Tale* as an extended meditation on the nature of love and what it truly entails. One of the points I find most valuable about the novel is a small scene in which the narrator is told a fable about a man named Trishanku. As I write in the essay, in the tale, Trishanku asks Brahma (the creator in Hindu tradition) about *Samsara*, the cycle of life-death-rebirth—reincarnation or the wheel of Being. Brahma assures that he will tell Trishanku what *Samsara* is, but only after Trishanku brings him a pillow on which to sit. Trishanku embarks on this seemingly small mission, only to be sidetracked from his goal by life itself. He meets a woman, significantly named Lila, which means "divine play" in Sanskrit, and we are made aware that the life that ensues for Trishanku, which is in essence Brahma's very lesson about *Samsara*, is in itself both the playfulness of the divine and the play (as in theater) the divine watches. Trishanku marries Lila, raises a family, finds worldly success, and then sees all swept away in a flood, his family and property gone. Unsure if he even wants to live, Trishanku suddenly finds the flood gone and sees "Brahma in a sea, a miracle, of light. He was a little impatient now, tapping his foot. 'Trishanku,' asked the Most High, 'where is my pillow?'" (Johnson 2005, 34)

The tale is both tragic and humorous, and it suggests that our efforts to fulfill the desires we have in life—desires for family or material comfort, and so on—can distract us from the larger purpose (or dharma to use the book's Buddhist bent) we're meant to enact; after all, Trishanku was asked to be of service to Brahma by bringing him a pillow so that he could then receive an answer to his question about the meaning of life. In some ways, then, we might read the parable as suggesting that if we are to find the meaning of life, we need to fulfill a role of service, regardless of whether that service occurs through the station of householder or sequestered monk. Additionally, the Trishanku story does not suggest that desires are bad or wrong, but it reminds us that they, based as they are in self-centered Ego, can distract us from that larger purpose of service. When the Ego's desires are prioritized, self-serving endeavors take precedence over the serving of others.

But what does this idea of service really mean, and why do so many spiritual traditions place it at the forefront of a life of virtue? Perhaps more importantly, we might wonder how we can ensure a life of service doesn't sink us into a state of enslavement.

Again, I find Johnson's novel offering readers interesting answers to these questions, especially since it is a neo-slave narrative and, as such, considers how to free its protagonist from every form of enslavement. Late in the novel, the protagonist Andrew is asked by his wife Peggy, "Can you . . . still love and believe in something when it's so beautiful it blinds you, and you *know* you can't have it? . . . You start feeling that goodness and beauty are for other people. For men, if you're a woman. Whites, if your [*sic*] nonwhite. Even the simple things—especially the simple things—like being wanted for yourself. To keep from feeling like waste, or destroying yourself, you have to destroy them. Deny them *here*" (Johnson 2005, 143), she says while touching his chest. Andrew will later answer his wife's question of how one can survive the sacrifice entailed in loving, but at this point, the novel attests that these limited and utterly human understandings and practices of love are destructive; what we typically call love causes suffering when one attempts to possess—and thereby objectify—the focus of that love.

Ultimately, this is not love at all but enslavement. Love, according to the novel, is something else—something enacted in the name of a greater good, rather than simply issued toward a finite object of desire or in an effort toward self-gain. We see this articulated by Andrew's father-in-law, who wishes for his daughter and Andrew "what the Greeks called *arête*, 'doing beautifully what needs to be done'" (Johnson 2005, 137). Andrew, pondering this, realizes, "Virtue was doing beautifully what the moment demanded" (Johnson 2005, 139), an idea that offers the possibility of divorcing action from desire, service from reward, or perhaps more accurately stated, of creating "right action," another definition of dharma. Andrew discovers, "My dharma, such as it was, was that of the householder" (Johnson 2005, 147), and in the chapter significantly titled "In the Service of the Servant," he begins to serve the one he calls the lowest among us, the enslaved girl he loved when he was young, Minty. In so doing, Andrew's own desire slips, in his words, from "remembered desire . . . to a biblical grief . . . for both her damaged beauty and, within me, the inevitable exchange of passion for compassion" (Johnson 2005, 155). This is an important moment, as we know the links between passion and desire; yet passion has its linguistic roots in "suffering," and Andrew's acknowledgment indicates a shift from self-serving desire to compassion, meaning "to suffer with." Andrew begins to enact selfless service, *seva* in Sanskrit, doing beautifully that which needs to be done. In declaring to his wife Peggy that he has a debt to repay through his care of Minty, Andrew articulates the responsibility of serving as the path toward his freedom; additionally, he speaks of the need to honor and acknowledge the past—and the sacrifices people have made in the past—as essential to his present freedom from suffering. His remembrance is not laced with bitterness or the need for retribution; instead, Andrew feels indebted for the richness of Being into which he was born and recognizes that he can no longer "[squander] to a thousand forms of bondage the only station . . . from which [Being] might truly be served" (Johnson 2005, 172). Tellingly, this moment of enacted dharma/Dharma, when he undertakes the service of the servant, initiates Andrew's liberation and, as such, seems to me to be the heart of the novel.

I love that novel, not only for the poetry of Johnson's language but also for its wisdom on love and service. Sometimes I remember arête when I don't want to clean the kitchen or play another board game with my daughter. And so the message becomes not only one about love and service but also about love and the growth that comes when we stretch beyond our momentary comforts toward something more enduring.

GROWTH

We can say, then, that another thing we must do for love is grow. And this growth is more than just the acceptance that there is housework to be done; it's a growth that can change and enliven our relationships and thereby our communities. If we are intentional about growth, we can move beyond our habitual ways of interacting with people and work to approach each encounter fresh and with open eyes—with nonjudgmental present moment awareness. By that, I mean that we can work to meet each person in the moment in which we find ourselves, rather than projecting other people, experiences, or times onto the one at hand. And with open eyes, we mindfully interact so that we are not simply reacting from our pre-programmed behavior.

In order to expand on this idea, I'd like to tell you about a conversation I had with a student, which ultimately was about the art and practice of connection. Our conversation occurred late in the spring, after our class had enjoyed a semester that included multiple intimate conversations with Rodney Hurst, local civil rights legend and activist. The class had researched Northeast Florida's civil rights history and its contemporary racial climate and, through a project spearheaded by my colleague Chris Janson, the students had interviewed local teachers who took part in Jacksonville's school desegregation efforts. This student and I were discussing how we can have mindful conversations on race. We began brainstorming a list of qualities that need to be individually developed in order for these conversations to be a productive part of anti-racist work:

- Surprisingly, the list for me began with anger, but a type of anger I was very specific about: righteous anger. This is not the anger that serves the self; rather, it is the anger that serves others. It's the anger that we feel when we see a wrong done to others that we insist be made right, and it is so often righteous anger that fuels social justice work.
- Curiosity, and more exactly a willingness to learn, came next. This is essential because we must know about the world that has existed and that now exists in order for us to envision how it should be.
- Awareness of our own ignorance. We must know that we don't know about a great deal in life—about others' realities and even our own unconscious processes. This awareness allows the humility that is necessary for ever-deeper learning.
- Bravery or moral courage is needed for us to speak up about injustice.
- Vulnerability is needed in order for us to open ourselves fully to the possibility of change, especially that in ourselves. And, as we've heard from Gandhi, we must be the change we wish to see in the world. In essence, we must be willing to change ourselves so that we come to embody within ourselves the world we wish to see outside of us. We must grow.
- Trust is needed, of course, in order for us to be vulnerable, but this doesn't necessarily mean trust in those with whom we feel at odds. It can simply mean trust in the necessity of something larger than ourselves—which might be called the greater good.

- A willingness to be uncomfortable is needed because, as discussed previously, no growth happens without discomfort.
- And collective leadership and action are required in order to organize multiple energies into a powerful force for change.

Such was our brainstorming (as well as my later contemplation). And it was in coming to the idea of collectivity, community, that we recognized the necessity of connection—in efforts to learn, in our openness to growth, in our commitment to justice. This collectivity demands connection, and the connection is alternately the product and the source of love. We all know about and typically hold a certain level of comfort with familial or romantic connection, yet connection might seem uncommon on a larger social scale. Still, I think we're seeing people crave this wider connection again, a connection that we may forget exists because we communicate so often through devices and distances, forgetting the important point that my colleague Jenni Lieberman notes: there are people on the other end of our phones and computers. I sometimes need to remind myself, as well, that there are people in those cars I want to honk at and speed past. And in our rush to "get there" (wherever that might be), we would do well to remember those are people checking us out at the supermarket. (Although we make this job obsolete with self-checkout, which is worth thinking about: in our effort to be quick and find convenience, we miss an opportunity for connection.)

Maybe we avoid or forget connection because it can be *so* uncomfortable, entailing as it does the vulnerability I just mentioned and leading as it so often does to the growth we might want to postpone. So how do we allow ourselves to be uncomfortable? How do we accept the invitation to growth that connection entails? How do we stay present in our interactions with others and embody arête in our lives?

To that end, I suggest regular Metta meditation practice, the Buddhist loving-kindness meditation offered in chapter 3 Mindfulness and Meditation Practices. As I note in that section, Metta is a practice that can help us live arête, finding the openheartedness to live our full potential.

CONCLUSION

I share that practice with you, knowing it is only one of many. As I mentioned earlier, every spiritual and religious tradition I can think of teaches the virtues of kindness, compassion, peace, service, doing unto others (and even unto the self) that which we want to be done to us—all of which can be rolled into that amorphous term LOVE.

I'll conclude by sharing a tiny poem that I think sums up very nicely the essence of love as service and the challenge love issues us to grow. It's by Hafiz (d. 1390), a Sufi poet of the fourteenth century:

Even after all this time,
The sun never says to the earth,
"You owe me."
Look what happens with a love like that—
It lights the whole sky. (Hafiz 1999, 34)

Just imagine the life-giving light we could shine if we were to love like that.

NOTE

1. See "Love and the Illusion of Race: Toward a Politics of Being" in *MELUS: Multi-ethnic Literature of the United States* 43:1 (Spring 2018): 183–213.

Afterword

From Conversation to Commitment

Andrew Woods

I would like to start a conversation from within privileged communities—a dialogue that refuses comfortable silence toward racial injustice. Let's also prioritize the exploration of *how* to respond in service and support of communities with less privilege.

The spark for this conversation is scandalous. At the University of North Florida (UNF) in Jacksonville, Florida, I learned a poignant history—Ax Handle Saturday. August 27, 1960, in downtown Jacksonville was brutal for African Americans, but the mainstream media documented none of it. If it did, maybe it would have become at least a bullet point in a U.S. history textbook? Or maybe not. The day began with the youth chapter of the local NAACP conducting lunch counter sit-ins for desegregation, with strict adherence to nonviolence in their protests. The youth were met with a 200-person mob of white men attacking African Americans downtown with axe handles and baseball bats, the police bystanders several blocks away.

Hearing this history, I was stunned. I listened in person to the stories of the still-local community members who helped organize the protest and who survived the attack. Admittedly, I had previously held the short-sighted perception that the civil rights movement is a period in somewhat distant history. But the men and women who shared their stories are barely a generation older than I am. *How* had I not heard about Ax Handle Saturday? Simply put, the Grade A school suburban neighborhoods I came up in were both separate and largely unconcerned with Jacksonville's core and underfunded districts.

This is why I want to start the conversation. People still suffer from racial oppression today; it often just looks different than the Jim Crow bullet points in our history textbooks. And before moving forward in conversation, I would like to propose we throw away the adjective "political," because "being political" is a poor description for the telling of a human being's story and a community's full history. The goal here is not political leverage. The goal is threefold: to recognize and understand the stories we've not been told, to overcome these stories' relegation to silence, and to respond justly, committing ourselves to work for better futures for all people. Again, we're talking about humans here, not agendas.

Rodney Hurst, the then president of the NAACP Youth Chapter and the leader of the sit-in demonstrations, writes in his book *It was never about a hot dog and a Coke*, "If we are committed to meaningful race relations in Jacksonville [and elsewhere], we must have serious dialogue and communication between the white community and the Black community" (Hurst 2008, 168). Applying this principle to any city, and to any cross-cultural relationships we form, we must ask *how* do we initiate this form of dialogue and communication?

Admittedly, I realize I may sound like an idealistic, privileged student, marching at issues that are rooted in centuries of racism, resilience, and recovery. Realistically, healing may take just as much time as the time spent inflicting wounds. But deciding to love our neighbors across cultural borders (even if change doesn't happen within our lifetime) is worth pursuing. We need to talk about *how* to make it happen and then take the steps to make it so.

Here's an idea that gives a more practical, less idea-based approach to a step forward. In an interview with Stephen Colbert, Killer Mike, who is a father, activist, and hip-hop artist, recommends the following to college students:

> Get outside the college environment, find a child who is marginal or doing exceptional in school, who's a minority—who doesn't look like you, not of the same religion, not of the same background. Help that child matriculate into college. Help them by being a big brother and big sister; help them by mentoring them. Don't give them gifts. Don't make yourself feel good like, "Hey! I gave 'em a new pair of sneakers!" Teach them the path you were taught to help them become a successful human being. What you're going to get out of that experience is another human being that's taking full advantage of an educational system that can help them and their community.

We have some practical ideas here for cross-cultural support. Find someone who is outside of your cultural bubble, don't settle for instant moral gratification, and commit to be a long-term ally within the context of a relationship. Although Killer Mike doesn't offer much specificity to address *how* to begin building the bridge, we have an idea. So in starting a conversation about *how* to serve communities, I want to share a story of my own.

Becoming a second grader's reading mentor seemed like a step in the right direction for me, but I recognize the approach needs some work. In a community-based learning course at UNF, I and about twenty classmates analyzed the importance of literacy while volunteering at an underfunded elementary school. Here's the program's strength: it listens to a community's needs and steps in to help fulfill it. At the same time, it revealed to my classmates and me how our grade school educations are rooted in privilege. However, the program fell short in its brevity. We developed relationships with the second-grade children for a semester, and then we left. Thankfully, the university continues to foster its relationship with the elementary school, but the kids who thrive with relational, one-on-one support see people come and go. We have the cross-cultural engagement, we have the relationship, but we lack the radical, long-term commitment to supporting a community—a commitment that could be transformational for all involved.

So, again, *how* do we begin forming committed relationships between communities? *How* do we form and sustain relationships across cultural borders? By sharing stories of successes and failures, we might create a network of testimonies to encourage one another to keep speaking up against and responding to the injustices we see today. More voices lend more perspective, giving us a more holistic understanding of the truth—and what we are committed to do when we hear it.

Appendix A

How to Be a Trojan Horse: Intervening in Racist Conversations

INTRODUCTION

As more work is done to understand and combat institutional and systemic racism, we are also invited to think through interpersonal relations and determine ways to interrupt and intervene in racist conversations. We might seek answers to the question *How do we begin the conversation that gets racists to rethink their attitudes and, ideally, alter their actions?* What do we do when a relative is making unacceptable comments in front of the TV or a roommate's jokes cross the line?

One thing is clear, racist conversations often happen when the target group is not present, so intervening in these conversations often means intervening in your own community or family. The good news is that there is a definite advantage to being perceived as a group member; you become a Trojan horse behind enemy lines, able to do much more than you could outside the walls.

So, how do we arm ourselves for interruption and then engagement of the issues?

NAVEL GAZING

The first step in most issues of diversity involves the old axiom of gazing into your navel; literally, learning what's within. Here are some questions to get you started:

a. What have been the major influences that have helped shape your racial identity?

b. When have you benefited from unearned privileges (being able-bodied, white, heterosexual, etc.) in your life?
c. What experiences have you had being in the minority? How did these experiences make you feel?
d. What are your internal biases and stereotypes about other groups?
e. What do you do when you see or hear someone being discriminated against?

SELF-AWARENESS TO ISSUE AWARENESS

We may have some self-reflectivity on our own standpoint regarding race and privilege, but we also need an understanding of racism itself.

To Do:
→ Without talking, write down your definition of racism.
→ Discuss as a group, finding a working definition for group conversation.

Racism is an overused word. There's a difference between the notion that *power + privilege = racism* and the idea that racism is the same as bigotry or discrimination. Our perceptions and experiences influence our definitions; multiply that difference by all the people in the world, and we begin to grasp how one person's racism can be another's party joke.

Is your friend being racist or is she being bigoted? Homing in on our definitions aids us in our approach. So we might ask, what does a racist comment or conversation sound like?

To Do:
→ Social barometer: Do you agree or disagree that the following statements are racist?

Welfare moms are lazy.
Affirmative action is reverse racism.
Asians are smart.
Interracial couples are wrong.
Mixed kids are so beautiful.
White people have no rhythm.
Latinos are the best lovers.
It's racist for all the black kids to sit together in the cafeteria.
There's nothing wrong with a sports team being called the "Redskins."

CHALLENGING RACISM AND OTHER FORMS OF OPPRESSION

a. *Challenge discriminatory attitudes and behavior.* Ignoring the issues will not make them go away and silence can send the message that you are in agreement with such attitudes and behaviors. Make it clear that you will not tolerate racial, ethnic, religious, or sexist jokes or slurs, or any actions that demean any person or group.
   → *How do we do that?*
   What works? "I" statements and questions more than criticism.
b. *Expect tension and conflict and learn to manage it.* Sensitive and deep-rooted issues are unlikely to change without some struggle and in many situations conflict is unavoidable. Face your fears and discomforts and remember that tension and conflict can be positive forces that foster growth.
   → *How do we do that?*
   Always protect your own physical, emotional, and mental health. If you're assured of your own safety, be prepared to be uncomfortable and move forward. As they say, "It's not about winning the battle; it's about winning the war." We don't need to fix everything in one conversation. Instead, we can build bridges that set the stage for deeper conversations later.
c. *Be aware of your own attitudes, stereotypes, and expectations.* Be open to discovering the limitations they place on your perspective. We have all been socialized to believe many myths and misconceptions and none of us remains untouched by the discriminatory messages in our society. Be honest with yourself about your own prejudices and biases. If you do not know something or are not sure how to handle a situation, say so and seek the information or help that you need. Practice not getting defensive when your own discriminatory attitudes or behaviors are pointed out to you.
   → *How do we do that?*
   Be self-reflective and dig deep when your own biases surface. Often biases come from ignorance, but just as often they come from social upbringing or misguided belief. If you've been told blue is green your whole life, it's hard to fault yourself for thinking that way. But once a truer perspective is pointed out, it's your responsibility to work thoroughly and possibly amend your individual norms. Likewise, just as you can be the holder of a misguided belief, so can others. Be hesitant to label someone as stupid or backward.
d. *Actively listen to and learn from others' experiences.* Don't minimize, trivialize, or deny people's concerns, and make an effort to see situations through their eyes.

→ *How do we do that?*

Develop your EQ! (your emotional quotient or emotional intelligence) Learn to practice empathy and try to stand in someone else's shoes. Consider what might make someone feel the need to verbally attack another; much bad behavior, except for that in sociopaths, is often based on fear. Try to be aware of others' realities and, as hard as it might be, put them at ease in your conversation. In order to challenge beliefs, we need to try to understand the root of the belief. It very likely is not hatred. And remember "both/and" thinking instead of "either/or." Believe it or not, your roommate *can* be both a bigoted person and a productive member of society.

e. *Use language and behavior that is unbiased and inclusive.* Develop this language for all people, regardless of race, ethnicity, sexuality, sex, ability, class, age, religion, and so forth.

→ *How do we do that?*

In other words, try to practice what you want to preach. Be true to your vision of community and, in Gandhi's words, "Be the change you wish to see in the world."

f. *Provide accurate information to challenge stereotypes and biases.* Take responsibility for educating yourself about your own and others' cultures. Do not expect people from different backgrounds to always educate you about their own culture or explain racism, sexism, and so on to you.

→ *How do we do that?*

Develop your social and cultural knowledge, replacing any guilt you might feel for your lack of awareness with the responsibility to educate yourself. Learn inclusive versions of history.

g. *Acknowledge diversity and avoid stereotypical thinking.* Don't ignore or pretend not to see our rich human differences. Acknowledging obvious differences is not the problem, but placing negative value judgments on those differences is. Stereotypes about those differences are harmful because they generalize, limit, and deny people's full humanity and individuality.

h. *Be aware of your own hesitancies to intervene.* Confront your own fears about interrupting discrimination, set your priorities, keep yourself safe, and take action. Develop response-ability!

→ *How do we do that?*

Acknowledge and allow for your own fears, but don't let emotions direct you away from standing your ground in defense of your values. Also, consider what "standing your ground" means for you. Walking out of a job because of discriminatory practices is a noble personal commitment but might not be the best choice for long-term change. As my colleague James Schuler reminded me, we don't need more people on the outside banging on the door. We need people on the inside making change happen there. People with privilege need to take a stand, but the stand might be remaining uncomfortable and working to help make positive changes.

i. *Project understanding, love, and support* when confronting individuals (as well as with the victims of attack). Without preaching, state how you feel and firmly address the hurtful behavior or attitude while supporting the dignity of every person. Be nonjudgmental in demeanor, if you can, but know the bottom line.

→ *How do we do that?*

Practice subversive love. Go against the social grain, be uncomfortable and socially imperfect, and confront what is often expected, allowed, or overlooked. Be unapologetically true to yourself and what you believe is right and just. It takes strength and self-love to do this, to follow your principles instead of the crowd you're in. But by befriending the "enemy," you can disarm them.

Appendix B
The Eight Limbs of Ashtanga Yoga

For those interested in learning more about yoga and its practices, the Eight Limbs, described in the Yoga Sutras of Patanjali, *are a useful introduction. Many of the ideas incorporated in this philosophy are applicable to discussions of mindfulness, community building, and "how to be" in the world and in relationship with others.*

ONE: The *Yamas* are restraints or abstinences. Nischala Joy Devi beautifully defines the *Yamas* as "reflections of our true nature." They are the qualities that are in harmony with and resonate from our deepest, truest self—that part of us that is in touch with the divine, with something larger than ourselves. Rolf Sovik, PhD, calls them "ethical restraints" and reminds us that they promote harmony in relationships; in other words, they help us remember what might be helpful or harmful in any given situation, helping us live peacefully with others and ourselves.

1) *Ahimsa* (nonviolence—gentleness and compassion)

   Although *ahimsa* is typically defined as nonviolence, I like to think of *ahimsa* as gentleness and compassion, for self and others. Seen in this way, *ahimsa* refers to how we treat those in our lives. It encourages you to think kind thoughts of yourself and others, to speak kind words to yourself and others. For some, *ahimsa* equates to being vegetarian or vegan. Is this the right path for you? If not, are there ways to make your eating gentler on the earth and other creatures, perhaps by eating organic or free-range or living more sustainably?

   Of course, *ahimsa* also means nonviolence and gentleness physically. Don't physically, emotionally, or mentally harm yourself or others, even with your practice of yoga *asana*. Don't feel like you have to twist yourself into a certain pose when you will only hurt yourself. Be gentle with your body. Be gentle with your emotions and mind. This means, too, that you're best off not comparing yourself with others, on and off the mat. It doesn't matter that your friend can do a headstand or touch her toes; what matters is how your body, mind, and spirit feel.

Ask yourself if you are working too hard to twist into a pose your body isn't ready to handle. Are you fighting your body? To answer these questions, consider your breath: Is it forced? uneven? ragged? are you holding it? Consider your face: Can you smile in this posture or are you frowning and grimacing? It's been said that violence and awareness can't coexist, so look inside and attend to yourself. Who you are and how you are is perfect right now. And by accepting what *is*, we make room for things to change for the better. Being gentle with yourself is a healthy way to grow.

2) *Satya* (truthfulness, integrity)

Speak truth: *the* truth, *your* truth. Be true to yourself. This takes courage and strength, an internal fire that is inextinguishable by external winds or the dampening energies of those who would seek to stifle you. When you are presented with choices in life, ask *Am I being honest with myself? With others? Is the choice I'm considering in alignment with my truth, with my beliefs and values?* Refrain from action until you know the answer is Yes.

Also, before speaking, ask the following three questions of what you're about to say:

Is it true?

In his book *The Four Agreements*, Don Miguel Ruiz advises, "Be impeccable with your word." Speaking the truth is so important. You are building your life with the words you say. If you remember that what you say influences what you think (and vice versa) and that what you think influences how you act, and that how you act shapes your experiences in life, then you'll realize the importance of speaking truthfully. Words are a building block of reality. Be honorable with them.

Is it kind?

Kindness and compassion are central tenets of yoga. Why? The science of yoga contends that every being is connected to every other being on the planet, human and nonhuman. What you do to others, then, is really what you do to yourself. Most major religions share this belief in one form or another as well. "Do unto others as you would have them do unto you." "And it harm none, do what you will." Even doctors recite an oath to this effect: "First, do no harm." Clearly, being kind is important, and frankly, it feels better.

Is it necessary?

Speaking is a huge drain of energy. Be careful and conscious of where you invest your energy. If something doesn't need to be said, it's usually better to hold your tongue. Many people spend so much time talking and very little time *doing* the things they talk about or *being* who they say they are or really *listening* to others; don't be one of them. Keep in mind the saying, "Those who speak, don't know. Those who know, don't speak."

Still, you need to prepare yourself for when speaking your truth is necessary, and you need to discern your truth as well. One way to really home in on your truth and develop the strength of your throat chakra—which is related to communication, sound, and self-expression—is through the practice of chanting. What you chant really doesn't matter as long as you feel comfortable enough to do it. You might begin simply by chanting a word from your spiritual tradition—*Om*, *Shalom*, or *Amen*, for example. Or a word that has special meaning to you like *peace* or *love*. Singing, too, opens up the throat chakra. So sing along to the radio, sing in the shower if you're shy; just exercise your voice so that when you do need to speak your truth, you'll be strong enough to do it.

3) *Asteya* (non-stealing—contentment and gratitude)

Asteya is known as "non-stealing." Though few of us can admit to being outright thieves, there are a number of ways in which we can rethink the things we might be taking from others:

Are you stealing time from your employer?

Are you stealing ideas from your classmates?

Are you stealing from yourself, robbing yourself of necessary time and energy for what's most important to you?

Are you keeping the extra money the cashier accidentally gave you?

Those of us who can answer "no" to the aforementioned questions can still broaden our understanding of *asteya* by imagining that it also entails cultivating a sense of contentment, peace, and gratitude for what we do have. Additionally, in order to practice true gratitude, we can offer thanks for the good that comes to others' lives. This can be hard to do sometimes, especially if we see others reaping what we've hoped to grow in our own lives. But because gratitude is the open door to abundance, being grateful for others' blessings as well as our own invites ever more goodness into our lives. And perhaps it serves as a sort of prayer, asking for more abundance to be brought to them as well. If the metaphysical maxim that "like attracts like" is true, then fostering positive thoughts, energy, and thankfulness will draw more positivity to us. Conversely, dwelling in a state of envy or jealousy will serve only to make us aware of and draw more negativity to us. The choice seems like a no-brainer, doesn't it?!

In our yoga practice, we can focus on prostrations (forward bends), which bring our head below our heart. The energy of these postures is to subsume our over-thinking, unsatisfied brains below our hearts, the organ that is the seat of contentment and gratitude. We can rest in restorative postures, finding ease and comfort with what *is*, rather than seeking to change, adjust, and always find something new. Instead of constantly moving, we can rest in the reality of what is present and allow a sense of acceptance to unfold.

4) *Brahmacharya* (moderation)

All work and no play? All play and no rest? Check in with yourself. Are you eating too much unhealthy food? Do you have too much stimulation from TV, music, or the computer? Be aware of what your body, mind, and spirit are taking in; you know when enough is enough.

Remember to eat nutritious foods and drink plenty of water. How much? Take your body weight; divide it in half. That is roughly how many *ounces* of water you need per day.

Get enough sleep; some experts say seven to nine hours per night is optimum.

Smile. Laugh. Dance. Sing. Think positive thoughts. Sometimes, stop thinking and just breathe. Be aware of how this feels.

5) *Aparigraha* (non-greed, non-hoarding)

Do you really need the latest and greatest electronic device? The trendy new shoes in the window? What really matters? Is there a better way to use your money, which is essentially energy in a material form? Is there something you could be saving for that would serve you better? Educational endeavors? A vacation? A house? Bills? Saving might not be as fun or flashy as spending right now, but it feels empowering to have the resources for what you really need later on.

TWO: The *Niyamas* are observances or practices that lead us ever deeper into our true nature, our highest self. Sovik calls them "actions to achieve self-balance." They are those practices that can lead us toward spiritual evolution and enlightenment, toward union with the divine.

1) *Saucha* (purity, cleanliness)

I remember learning something in a seventh-grade computer class that has stayed with me: "garbage in, garbage out." That is, what we put into something is the basis of what we will get out of it; that applies to everything: school, work, sports, *asana* practice, relationships, and our bodies.

We've all heard the saying, "You are what you eat," and this is another version of the same idea; what you feed your body (and your mind) is the source of what you get out of it.

So what does this mean for our lives? And what is purity exactly? We might define purity as something that is whole, healthful, clean, honest, and unadulterated. In the realm of food, people talk about whole foods rather than processed (fresh fruits and vegetables rather than boxed cereals or macaroni and cheese), and our bodies do well with the freshest, most whole food available to us.

But this idea of purity flows into other areas of our lives as well; it relates to not harboring ill-will or feeding unkind thoughts about others (or yourself). When you find yourself thinking unkind or unproductive thoughts, be aware of your thinking, and make a change. This can be through trying to find the positive in a person or situation or it can be simply hitting the "stop" button on the thoughts going through your head. Of course, these thoughts will probably return, but you can treat them the same way next time; eventually, they won't repeat themselves to you so often or with such force.

Purity and cleanliness matter in terms of our bodies and our minds, but they also matter in terms of what we choose to surround ourselves with. Keep your space clean—internally and externally—and clean up after yourself. Take care of any messes you make, in your home, your workplace, even your relationships.

2) *Santosha* (contentment)

This action pairs nicely with the restraint of *aparigraha* (non-grasping, non-hoarding). When we loosen our desire for material things or even for our life to be other than it is, we often find ourselves more happy, more content, and this can lead to truly positive changes in areas that are necessary. So remember as much as you're able to bloom where you're planted, love your life, live your life, and love the changes.

This acceptance and contentment doesn't mean that you don't strive for goals and dreams or that you remain complacent in the face of injustice; instead, it means accepting things as they are rather than fighting in your own head and heart for them to be otherwise. From this place of recognizing reality, of present moment awareness, you'll be able to strive for real change in the world around you.

Really, this means that even if there are things in yourself or your life you want to change, accepting things as they are right now—in this moment—will give you the right attitude, ideas, and emotions to move toward something better. It's when we don't accept what is that we remain stuck—fighting with our own minds and wasting energy on frustration. We're most efficient when we work with the positive. We have

better control with an open palm than a closed fist, so we can welcome necessary change by accepting our starting point.
3) *Tapas* (austerity, discipline, zeal for practice)

Patanjali, a sage revered by many yogis, says that a yogic practice is well grounded when it is practiced *consistently*, over a long time, and in all earnestness. We can bring this idea to bear on the rest of our lives as well; whatever is worth doing is worth doing well. If you choose to invest your time and energy in something, do so whole-heartedly. Be diligent, be disciplined, be motivated—or don't do it! Find the things you feel this passionately about, and invest yourself wisely; today is the only day you have, so don't be a dabbler; be a practitioner, a student, a "disciple." It's from this word that we take the work discipline, reminding us that we have to be dedicated to those things that matter to us.

4) *Svadhyaya* (self-study, study of scriptures)

There will always be more to know—about the world, about life, about yourself. Practice humility in the face of this immense knowledge, and strive to know more. Ask questions. Seek answers, in formal and informal ways. Read and study, but also pay attention to the lessons life teaches; look for signs and synchronicity; recognize there are no mistakes and there is a lesson in every experience; remember that each being you encounter is your teacher.

Remember, too, that the "holy" or inspired texts of spiritual traditions can teach you much; they can help answer your questions and guide you in living. So can your own heart and your truest self. Read and then meditate. Your truth will resonate within you.

5) *Ishwara Pranidhana* (surrender to divine will, if that is your belief; surrender to something higher than the self)

Recognize that you do not have control over much in life. At the same time, remember that you create your life every day. Your life is a garden, and each thought is a flower or a weed. Plant flowers, and watch your garden bloom, overflowing with variety and color. We are not the ones who bring rain and sunshine, storms and seed-scattering wind. Enjoy every season and every element, since they all have their purpose. Be creative in your garden, sow what you want to grow, then let go and let life flow.

THREE: *Asana*

These are the yoga poses themselves, and there are thousands of them, given quaint names like rabbit and turtle in English or exotic sounding Sanskrit names like *Padangusthasana* and *Matsyendrasana*. *Asana* is good for the body, as it helps us develop strength, flexibility, and balance. After *asana* practice, which can feel as invigorating as aerobic exercise and as soothing as a massage, we find our mind is clearer, our senses sharper, our bodies more efficient. *Asana* can be treated like exercise (you can definitely work up a sweat and tone your muscles), but it is also a meditation fostered through movement and stillness, through transitioning from one pose to another and then holding that pose long enough to allow our bodies and minds to make adjustments. *Asana* involves awareness of what is going on inside of you, not anywhere beyond your yoga mat. How is your breath during your *asana* practice? Jagged and labored, through your mouth? Or is it smooth and fluid, deep and even, through your nose? We work toward the latter in *asana* practice, and we tune into the sensations within the body. You will develop awareness of subtle currents of energy in the body, and these—along with your breath—will guide your practice. It's helpful to find a reputable, certified yoga instructor to teach you and help you learn alignment within the poses, but remember that you are ultimately your best teacher. Your yoga teacher will offer you suggestions during your practice, but you must also listen to your own body and breath; you will teach yourself well.

FOUR: *Pranayama* (breath exercise)
Control of the breath helps us steady and calm the mind, which is a major component of yoga. Not only that, *pranayama*, which literally means restraint (*yama*) of prana (*energy*), helps on the most subtle energetic levels. This is why mindful awareness of the breath is a meditation technique, calming the mind and relieving stress in the body. Various breath exercises can be used to increase energy or relax the body, to increase lung capacity and strengthen the immune system, to decrease hypertension and improve focus and concentration. Breath exercises are usually accessible for most bodies, so they can be a beneficial entrée into other yoga and meditation practices.

FIVE: *Pratyahara* (sense withdrawal)
Turning inward is necessary for both healing and growth; you are aware that seeds lie dormant during winter, storing energy for the right time to bloom. You know that bears hibernate, conserving their resources for the next time of plenty. In this way, much within nature demonstrates to us the benefit of turning within. When we give ourselves time for such a practice, it is not so that we withdraw completely from society or interaction, as a monk might. Instead, we turn inward so that we can hear our own true self resonating in the midst of what is often the omnipresent distraction of culture. We are constantly seeing, hearing, tasting, touching, smelling everything around us, and we can become overstimulated and overwhelmed by all of this sensory information. Taking a break from some of these energy drains—like the TV or radio—can be highly refreshing and encourage new awareness within ourselves. Give yourself time—daily if you can—to remove yourself from

the cultural distractions that pervade your environment. Turn off the TV, put down your cell phone, take some time to breathe. Go outside for a walk. Write in a journal. Practice meditation. When you return to your daily routine, you may find that your senses are sharper, you feel more alert and aware. You may hear yourself speaking inner truths. You may find inspiration and energy to take on new endeavors or pastimes. You may become a better listener for your friends. In any case, you will likely feel more relaxed and ready to tackle any challenges that await you.

Just as this practice of sense withdrawal is important in your life, it is also important during *asana* practice. When your senses are turned inward, you are no longer concerned with how you look in a pose compared to someone else in the room (or in your own imagination); instead, you are concerned with how you *feel* in a pose. Remember that you turn to the sensations in your body and breath to guide your *asana* practice, and this essentially entails *pratyahara*. When you don't allow yourself to be distracted by the music playing, the noises of cars outside the yoga studio, or even by the person practicing next to you, you will reap greater rewards from your *asana* practice and begin training your mind for mediation.

SIX: *Dharana* (concentration)
Because *asana* and *pranayama* demand our mind's attention, they help us increase our ability to concentrate, an ability that has numerous physiological, psychological, and emotional benefits in addition to practical benefits for daily life. Increased concentration means you can do what needs to be done in the most efficient way possible, preserving time and energy.

On an interpersonal level, increased focus means greater attention to those with whom we're in relationship. How many times have you seen a family at a restaurant, all plugged into their electronic devices and therefore not "plugged into" each other? Fostering a mind accustomed to concentration and focus can aid our relationships, freeing us from distractions and helping us have full awareness of and appreciation for the present moment and those with whom we share it.

SEVEN: *Dhyana* (meditation)
It has been said that *asana* practice was created to make the body ready for long periods of seated meditation. It's certainly true that working the body through *asana*—increasing its strength, balance, flexibility, and endurance—can work out the kinks that might distract us when we hope to sit for meditation. All of the earlier practices help us prepare for the one-pointed focus of meditation, which—when practiced regularly, earnestly, and without ceasing—can lead us to Samadhi.

EIGHT: *Samadhi* (bliss, union)
The body and mind drop away and we rest in pure being. This abstract description is the best I can offer, because Samadhi can be experienced but cannot adequately be described. This state of bliss and union with "what is" might be experienced in glimpses throughout life; athletes call it being in "the zone," when they are at one with their bodies, their task. You might have enjoyed other experiences that brought you the same immersion in the present moment. And meditation can take you there as well. Samadhi is the state of being many strive to reach. Numerous people do reach it fleetingly. How wonderful it would be to live there.

Appendix C
Benefits of Asana, Pranayama, *and Meditation*

BENEFITS OF *ASANA* (PHYSICAL POSTURES)

Physiological

- Autonomic nervous system equilibrium stabilizes
- Pulse rate decreases
- Respiration rate decreases
- Blood pressure decreases
- Cardiovascular efficiency increases
- Respiratory efficiency increases
- Gastrointestinal function normalizes
- Endocrine function normalizes
- Excretory functions improve
- Musculoskeletal flexibility and joint range of motion increase
- Breath retention time increases
- Joint range of motion increases
- Grip strength increases
- Eye-hand coordination improves
- Dexterity improves
- Reaction time improves
- Posture and balance improve
- Strength and resiliency increase
- Endurance and energy level increase
- Weight normalizes
- Sleep improves
- Immunity increases
- Pain decreases

- Steadiness improves
- Depth perception improves
- Integrated functioning of body parts improves

Psychological

- Somatic and kinesthetic awareness increase
- Mood improves and subjective well-being increases
- Self-acceptance and self-actualization increase
- Social adjustment increases
- Anxiety and depression decrease
- Hostility decreases
- Concentration improves
- Memory and attention improve
- Learning efficiency improves

Biochemical

- Glucose decreases
- Sodium decreases
- Total cholesterol decreases
- Triglycerides decrease
- HDL cholesterol increases
- LDL cholesterol decreases
- Cholinesterase increases
- Hematocrit and hemoglobin increase
- Lymphocyte count increases
- Total white blood cell count decreases
- Vitamin C and thyroxin increase
- Total serum protein increases

BENEFITS OF *PRANAYAMA* (BREATHING EXERCISES)

Physiological

- Immune system strengthens
- Lung capacity increases
- Efficient use of oxygen in the body increases
- Physical control of the body increases
- Body is purified and detoxified
- Energy flow in the body increases

- Metabolic and endocrine systems balance
- Nervous system is cleansed and toned
- Pain caused by compression of nerve endings soothes
- Respiratory system strengthens
- Blood oxygenated and residual carbon dioxide in lungs purged
- Organ function improves
- Digestion improves
- Hypertension decreases
- ATP production (chemical basis of energy production in the body) increases

Psychological

- Mind calms and steadies
- Focus and concentration improve
- Emotional control and equilibrium improve
- Stress reduces

BENEFITS OF MEDITATION

Physiological

- Metabolic rate decreases
- Heart rate lowers and work load of heart decreases
- Deep rest is realized
- Autonomic nervous system stabilizes
- Cortisol and lactate (two stress-related chemicals) levels decrease
- Free radicals (unstable oxygen molecules that cause tissue damage) decrease
- Activity in the frontal cortex and parietal lobe decrease
- Left and right brain coordination increases
- Theta waves, delta waves, and alpha waves increase in activity and beta wave activity decreases
- Production of serotonin increases
- Blood pressure decreases
- Endocrine functions improve
- Skin resistance increases (low skin resistance is correlated with higher stress and anxiety levels)
- Cholesterol decreases
- Stability improves
- Electromyographic (EMG) activity increases
- Air flow to the lungs improves

- Aging process slows
- Dehydroepiandrosterone (DHEAS; associated with youthfulness) in the elderly increases

Psychological

- Brain wave coherence increases
- Creativity increases
- Anxiety and depression decrease
- Irritability and moodiness decrease
- Learning ability and memory improve
- Self-actualization and self-acceptance increase
- Feelings of vitality and rejuvenation increase
- Happiness increases
- Emotional stability increases
- Relaxation response increases
- Concentration, memory, and attention improve
- Self-discipline increases

Appendix D
Foundational Yoga Postures

Appendix D

Figure D.1 Foundational Yoga Postures. David M. Hall.

Appendix E
Resources

FACILITATING DIFFICULT CONVERSATIONS AND CIVIC DISCOURSE

- Center for Ethical Leadership—http://www.ethicalleadership.org/
- Handbook for Facilitating Difficult Conversations in the Classroom—https://teach.ufl.edu/wp-content/uploads/2016/07/Handbook-for-Facilitating-Difficult-Conversations2.pdf
- Kettering Foundation—https://www.kettering.org/
- National Institute for Civil Discourse—https://nicd.arizona.edu/
- *Race Dialogues: A Facilitator's Guide to Tackling the Elephant in the Classroom* by Donna Rich Kaplowitz et. al.

HOLISTIC TEACHING AND CREATIVITY

- Carnegie Foundation for the Advancement of Teaching—https://www.carnegiefoundation.org/
- Creative assignments: artist journals—https://andrewkozlowski.domains.unf.edu/Italy2019/books/
- Creating Critical Reflection Assignments—https://www.pugetsound.edu/academics/experiential/create-experiential-learning-opportunities/available-resources/creating-critical-reflection-assignments/
- *Syllabus* by Lynda Barry
- *A Big New Free Happy Unusual Life* by Nina Wise
- *The Artist's Way* by Julia Cameron

MINDFULNESS

- Association for Contemplative Mind in Higher Education—https://acmhe.org
- Insight Timer App (Meditation and yoga)—insighttimer.com
- Koru Mindfulness (Meditation for college-aged students)—korumindfulness.org
- Positive Psychology—positivepsychology.com
- *Trauma Sensitive Mindfulness* by David Treleaven
- University of Massachusetts Memorial Medical Center—Center for Mindfulness—https://www.umassmemorialhealthcare.org/umass-memorial-medical-center/services-treatments/center-for-mindfulness

SELF-CARE AND SOMATICS

- Academics for Black Survival and Wellness—https://www.academics4blacklives.com/
- Harvard University Anti-Racism Resources—https://projects.iq.harvard.edu/antiracismresources/bipoc/selfcare
- *My Grandmother's Hands: Racialized Trauma and the Pathway to Mending Our Hearts and Bodies* by Resmaa Menakem
- POC Online Classroom—https://www.poconlineclassroom.com/self-care
- *The Body Is Not an Apology: The Power of Radical Self-Love* by Sonya Renee Taylor
- *The Politics of Trauma: Somatics, Healing, and Social Justice* by Staci K. Haines

SOCIAL JUSTICE

- Teaching Tolerance—tolerance.org
- Learning for Justice—https://www.learningforjustice.org/
- Revolutionary Love Project—(https://valariekaur.com/revolutionary-love-project/)

YOGA

- Yoga International—https://yogainternational.com
- Yoga Alliance—yogaalliance.org
- Yoga Journal—yogajournal.com

Bibliography

Adams, Susan R. and Jamie Buffington-Adams. *Race & Pedagogy: Creating Collaborative Spaces for Teacher Transformations*. Lanham: Lexington Books, 2016.

Al-Atiyat, Ibtesam. "Tackling the "Savior" Complex: Teaching Introduction to Women's and Gender Studies through Deliberation." In *Deliberative Pedagogy: Teaching and Learning for Democratic Engagement*, edited by Shaffer, Timothy J., et al., n.p. Lansing: Michigan State UP, 2017. EBSCOhost.

Baer, Rebecca. "Why Diversity Matters in the B-School Classroom." Graduate Management Admission Council. 10 Jan. 2018. https://www.mba.com/business-school-and-careers/diversity-and-inclusion/diversity-matters-in-b-school

Barry, Lynda. *Syllabus: Notes from an Accidental Professor*. Montreal: Drawn & Quarterly, 2019.

Baston, C. Daniel. "The Empathy-Altruism Hypothesis." In *Empathy: From Bench to Bedside*, edited by Jean Decety, 41–54. Cambridge: MIT Press, 2012.

Beals, Emily. "Mindfulness Conversations, Episode 2: Asao Inoue. *YouTube*, 1 May 2020, https://www.youtube.com/watch?v=QHkPacjwKjY

Blackwell, Deanna M. "Sidelines and separate spaces: Making education anti-racist for students of color." *Race, Ethnicity, and Education*, 13, no. 4 (2010), 473–494. DOI: 10.1080/13613324.2010.492135.

Borsheim-Black, Carlin and Sophia Tatiana Sarigianides. *Letting Go of Literary Whiteness: Antiracist Literature Instruction for White Students*. New York: Teachers College Press, 2019.

Brammer, Leila R. "Deliberative Pedagogy as a Central Tenet: First-Year Students Develop a Course and a Community." In *Deliberative Pedagogy: Teaching and Learning for Democratic Engagement*, edited by Timothy Shaffer, et al., n.p. Lansing: Michigan State University Press, 2017. EBSCOhost.

Brown, Brené. "The Power of Vulnerability." TED Talk. 4 March 2014. https://www.ted.com/talks/brene_brown_the_power_of_vulnerability/transcript?language=en

Bruner, Jerome. "Narrative, Culture, and Mind." In *Telling Stories: Language, Narrative, and Social Life*, edited by Anastasia Nylund, et al., 45–49. Washington, D.C.: Georgetown University Press, 2010.

Carillo, Ellen C. *A Writer's Guide to Mindful Reading*. Boulder: University Press of Colorado, 2017.

Carnegie https://compact.org/initiatives/carnegie-community-engagement-classification/

Coplan, Amy. "Empathic engagement with narrative fictions." *The Journal of Aesthetics and Art Criticism*, 62, no. 2 (Spring, 2004), 141–152.

"Creating Gracious Space Facilitator Guide Module One: Introduction to Gracious Space," Center for Ethical Leadership, accessed April 30, 2021, http://www.ethicalleadership.org/uploads/2/6/2/6/26265761/gs_overview.pdf

Crenshaw, Kimberle. "Mapping the Margins: Intersectionality, Identity Politics, and Violence against Women of Color." *Stanford Law Review*, 43, no. 6 (Jul 1991), 1241–1299.

Darder, Antonia and Rodolfo D. Torres. "Shattering the 'Race' Lens: Toward a Critical Theory of Racism." In *Critical Ethnicity: Countering the Waves of Identity Politics*, edited by Robert H. Tai and Mary L. Kenyatta, 173–192. Lanham: Rowman & Littlefield, 1999.

Davis, Dannielle Joy and Patricia G. Boyer. *Social Justice Issues & Racism in the College Classroom*. Bingley: Emerald Group Publishing, 2013.

Dery, Mark. "Black to the Future." In *Flame Wars: The Discourse of Cyberculture*, edited by Mark Dery, 179–222. Durham: Duke, 1994.

Devi, Nischala Joy. *The Secret Power of Yoga: A Woman's Guide to the Heart and Spirit of the Yoga Sutras*. New York: Three Rivers Press, 2007.

DiAngelo, Robin. *White Fragility: Why It's So Hard for White People to Talk about Racism*. Boston: Beacon Press, 2018.

"Diversity as an Engine of Innovation," Deloitte, accessed April 30, 2021, https://www2.deloitte.com/us/en/insights/deloitte-review/issue-8/diversity-as-an-engine-of-innovation.html

Ellis, Trey. *Platitudes and "The New Black Aesthetic."* Boston: Northeastern UP, 2003. "Employment Projections: 2019–2029," United States Bureau of Labor Statistics, accessed May 14, 2021, https://www.bls.gov/news.release/pdf/ecopro.pdf

Enos, S. & Morton, K. "Developing a Theory and Practice of Campus-Community Partnerships." In *Building Partnerships for Service Learning*, edited by B. Jacoby and Associates, 20–41. Hoboken: John Wiley & Sons, 2003.

"Falling Short? College Learning and Career Success," Hart, accessed April 30, 2021, https://www.aacu.org/sites/default/files/files/LEAP/2015employerstudentsurvey.pdf

Fanon, Frantz. *Black Skin, White Masks*. New York: Grove Press, 1952.

Frawley, David. *Mantra Yoga and Primal Sound*. Detroit: Lotus Press, 2010.

Ganz, Marshall. "Why Stories Matter: The Art and Craft of Social Change." *Sojourners* (March 2009), https://sojo.net/magazine/march-2009/why-stories-matter

Gates, Henry Louis, Jr. *The Signifying Monkey: A Theory of African-American Literary Criticism.* New York: Oxford UP, 1988.
Guajardo, Miguel A., et al. *Reframing Community Partnerships in Education: Uniting the Power of Place and the Wisdom of People.* Philadelphia: Routledge, 2016.
Hafiz. 1999. *The Gift: Poems by Hafiz, The Great Sufi* Master. Translated by Daniel Ladinsky. London: Penguin Compass.
Haviland, V. "'Things get glossed over': Rearticulating the silencing power of whiteness in education." *Journal of Teacher Education,* 59, no. 1 (2008), 40–54.
hooks, bell. *Teaching Community: A Pedagogy of Hope.* Philadelphia: Routledge, 2003.
"How do we overcome our differences?" National Institute for Civil Discourse, accessed June 19, 2020, https://www.engagingdifferences.org
Hurst, Rodney L. *It Was Never About a Hot Dog and a Coke.* Livermore: WingSpan Press, 2008.
Irvine, Judith T., and Susan Gal. "Language, ideology, and linguistic differentiation." In *Regimes of Language: Ideologies, Polities, and Identities,* edited by Paul V. Kroskrity, 35–84. Santa Fe: School of American Research Press, 2000.
Johnson, Charles. *Oxherding Tale.* New York: Scribner, 2005.
———. *Taming the Ox: Buddhist Stories and Reflections on Politics, Race, Culture, and Spiritual Practice.* Boulder: Shambhala, 2014.
Kaur, Valarie. *See No Stranger: A Memoir and Manifesto of Revolutionary Love.* London: One World, 2020.
Keen, Suzanne. "A theory of narrative empathy." *Narrative,* 14, no. 3 (2006), 207–236, accessed March 16, 2021. https://www.jstor.org/stable/20107388
Kernahan, Cyndi. *Teaching about Race: Race and Racism in the College Classroom: Notes from a White Professor.* Morgantown: West Virginia UP, 2019.
Kolb, D.A. *Experiential Learning: Experience as the Source of Learning and Development.* Englewood Cliffs, NJ: Prentice Hall, 1984.
L'Engle, Madeleine. *A Circle of Quiet.* New York: Harper & Row, 1972.
Leverette, Tru. "Love and the Illusion of Race: Toward a Politics of Being." *MELUS: Multi-Ethnic Literature of the United States,* 43, no. 1 (Spring 2018), 183–213.
Levin, Janina. "Productive dialogues across differences: Literature and empathy studies." *Journal of Modern Literature,* 39, no. 4 (Summer 2016), 187–193, accessed March 15, 2021. https://www.jstor.org/stable/10.2979/jmodelite.39.4.14
Lilla, Mark. "How Colleges are Strangling Liberalism." *Chronicle of Higher Education,* August 20, 2017. http://www.chronicle.com/article/How-Colleges-Are-Strangling/240909?key=_ds5xEy29SM9Wq4Ek8CmAQtrc-CeIrKfiAiM9xrC72o wFjxGcKz7IMnqil4QSloiYk84ZDk1Tm12cVVDUE5LTU91RFhNNW1JeV h0VVhUdllEVlBtMG9zemI5MA.
Love, Bettina L. "Difficulty knowledge: When a black feminist educator was too afraid to #SayHerName." *English Education,* 49, no. 2 (2017), 197–208.
Mathews, David. "Forward." In *Deliberative Pedagogy: Teaching and Learning for Democratic Engagement,* edited by Timothy J. Shaffer, et al., n.p. Lansing: Michigan State University Press, 2017.

Menakem, Resmaa. *My Grandmother's Hands: Racialized Trauma and the Pathway to Mending Our Hearts and Bodies.* Las Vegas: Central Recovery Press, 2017.

Okun, Tema. *The Emperor Has No Clothes: Teaching about Race & Racism to People who Don't Want to Know.* Charlotte: Information Age Publishing, 2010.

Olumide, Jill. *Raiding the Gene Pool: The Social Construction of Mixed Race.* Sterling: Pluto Press, 2002.

Ragoonaden, Karen, ed. *Mindful Teaching and Learning: Developing a Pedagogy of Well-Being.* Lanham: Lexington Books, 2015.

"Reggie Hubbard - Active Peace Yoga," *Yoga Unify*, accessed March 5, 2021. yogaunify.org/yoga-u-directory/active-peace-yoga/

Ruiz, Don Miguel. *The Four Agreements: A Practical Guide to Personal Freedom.* San Rafael: Amber-Allen, 1997.

Schiffrin, Deborah and Anna De Fina. "Introduction." In *Telling Stories: Language, Narrative, and Social Life*, edited by Anastasia Nylund, 1–6. Washington, D.C.: Georgetown UP, 2010.

Shaffer, Timothy J. "Democracy and Education: Historical Roots of Deliberative Pedagogy." In *Deliberative Pedagogy: Teaching and Learning for Democratic Engagement*, edited by Timothy J. Shaffer, et al., n.p. Lansing: Michigan State University Press, 2017. EBSCOhost.

Shetty, Malavika. "Identity Building through Narratives on a Tulu Call-in TV Show." In *Telling Stories: Language, Narrative, and Social Life*, edited by Anastasia Nylund, et al., 95–108. Washington, D.C.: Georgetown University Press, 2010.

Sovik, Rolf. *Moving Inward: The Journey to Meditation.* Honesdale: Himalayan Institute, 2005.

Strachan, J. Cherie. "Deliberative Pedagogy's Feminist Potential: Teaching Our Students to Cultivate a More Inclusive Public Sphere." In *Deliberative Pedagogy: Teaching and Learning for Democratic Engagement,* edited by Timothy J. Shaffer, et al., n.p. Lansing: Michigan State University Press, 2017. EBSCOhost.

Strand, Kerry, et al. *Community-Based Research and Higher Education.* San Francisco: Jossey-Bass, 2003.

Sue, Derald Wing. *Race Talk and the Conspiracy of Silence: Understanding and Facilitating Difficult Dialogues on Race.* Hoboken: Wiley, 2015.

Taylor, Sonya Renee. *The Body is Not an Apology.* Oakland: Berrett-Koehler Publishers, 2018.

"Train the Trainer Revised CCP 101 Class," University of North Florida Department of Diversity Initiatives, August 1, 2017.

TuSmith, Bonnie and Maureen T. Reddy (editors). *Race in the College Classroom: Pedagogy and Politics.* Piscataway: Rutgers UP, 2002."2019 Millennial Survey," Deloitte, accessed April 30, 2021, https://www2.deloitte.com/content/dam/Deloitte/global/Documents/About-Deloitte/deloitte-2019-millennial-survey.pdf

Vatrapu, Ravi K. "Cultural considerations in computer supported collaborative learning." *Research and Practice in Technology Enhanced Learning*, 3, no. 2 (2008), 1–42.

Walker, Alice. *Meridian.* San Diego: Harcourt, 1976.

Wheatley, M. J. "Some friends and I started talking. . . ." *UTNE Reader*, July/August 2002.

Wiggins, Grant. *Educative Assessment: Designing Assessments to Inform and Improve Student Performance*. San Francisco: Jossey-Bass, 1998.

Yoga Sutras of Patanjali. Trans. Sri Swami Satchidananda. Integral Yoga Publications, 1978.

Index

Page references for figures are italicized.

accommodations, 18, 44, 46, 62, 72, 78–79, 94
active listening, 23, 37–39, 54
Afrofuturism, 58–59
agency, xxi, 1, 8, 11, 30, 59
ally, xxii, 34, 40, 122
altruism, 55
anger, x, xvi, 1, 27, 31, 40, 56, 60, 117
arête, 63, 116, 118
argumentation, xvi, 1, 25–26
art, 87, 89–90, 97, 117
asana, xii, 131, 134, 136–38; benefits of, 141; mountain pose, 43–44, 48–49, 61; six movements of the spine, 16, 20; standing back bend, 61; tree pose, 77–78, 80–81

beloved community, xviii, 4, 30
bias, xx, xxii, 23, 25, 42, 47, 70, 126–28
Black Lives Matter, xvii
body, x–xiii, xxii–xxiii, 7, 16–21, 29, 31, 37, 43–44, 47–48, 61–62, 64–65, 77–78, 80, 88, 102, 106, 108, 132, 134–39, 142–43
bodies, x–xiii, xviii, xxii–xxiii, 2, 8–10, 19–20, 28, 48–49, 62, 83, 92, 101, 110, 114, 134–35, 137, 139
body scan. *See* meditation

breath, xi–xiii, xxii–xxiii, 16–21, 31, 43–45, 47–48, 64, 80, 132, 137–38, 141
breathing, xxii, 17, 19–21, 48, 64, 84, 92, 142; diaphragmatic, xii, 19, 47

civil discourse, xv–xvii, xx, 4, 24–26, 39
civil rights, 3–4, 51, 91, 94, 96–97, 102, 117; movement, 4–5, 7, 103, 111, 121
citizenship, 27, 42n1, 51, 67, 103, 110
cognitive dissonance, 11, 32
collaboration, 26, 29, 38, 68–69, 71, 73–74, 94
comfort, xii, 10, 17–18, 28–30, 42, 45, 62, 64, 80, 87, 91, 106, 115–16, 118, 121, 133–34
comfortable. *See* comfort
communication, xxiii, 41–42, 53, 72, 122, 133
community-based learning. *See* learning
community engagement, xix, xxi, 55, 60, 73, 93
Community Learning Exchange, 59
compassion, 29, 36, 40, 53, 55, 63, 75, 81, 114, 116, 118, 131–32
conflict, xx, 20, 21n2, 24, 32, 36, 52, 63–65, 72, 74, 84, 127

155

consensus, 23–26, 37, 46, 74
critical thinking, 24, 27, 68, 88
cultural competence, 69–72
culture, xv, xxiii, 1–4, 24, 29, 59, 65, 70–72, 84, 96, 102, 108, 110, 128, 137

deliberative pedagogy, xix–xx, 4, 9, 23–28
deliberation, 21n2, 24–26
democracy, xx, 24, 27, 67
dharma, xix, 115–16
dialogue, xvi, xix–xx, xxii, 9, 12, 21n2, 23–25, 27, 29, 31–32, 39, 42, 54, 85, 94, 121–22
diaphragm, 19
discomfort, xi–xii, 1, 10–11, 28–29, 33, 36–37, 39–40, 42n4, 48, 63, 87, 118, 127, 129
discourse, xv–xvii, xx, 4, 11, 13n9, 24–26, 39, 57, 67, 147
diversity and inclusion, xv, xvii, 28
drawing. *See* art

education, xxi, 7, 10, 24, 26–27, 34, 68–69, 73, 94, 98
empathic recognition, 55–56, 64
empathy, xix, xxi, 23, 27, 31, 40, 53–55, 57, 61, 64–65, 67, 71, 89, 92, 128; narrative, 54, 57
emotional contagion, 55
erasure, 58–59
equanimity, xii, 65, 75

Fanon, Franz, 4, 6
fear, xvi, xx, 31, 40, 53, 63, 107, 128

Gandhi, Mohandas, xviii, 117, 128
Gracious Space, 29, 42

holistic, ix, xvi, xxi–xxii, 68, 83, 87, 89–90, 123, 147

identity, xvi–xix, xxi, 2–9, 12n2, 34–36, 42, 55–57, 71, 74, 84–85, 101, 110, 125; politics, xviii, 2–9, 12n2, 34

image. *See* art
intersectionality, 3, 93

Kabat-Zinn, Jon, x
King, Martin Luther, Jr., xviii, 4, 7, 30, 112

language, 26, 31–33, 38–39, 53, 57, 72, 85, 108, 110, 116, 128; body, xxiii, 29, 37
learning, ix, xiii, xvi, xx–xxi, 11–12, 24–27, 29, 31, 33–34, 63, 67–69, 71–73, 85–86, 89–91, 93, 96, 111–12, 117, 125, 142, 144, 148; community-based, xix, xxi–xxii, 9, 68–69, 74, 76n2, 85, 93–94, 96, 123; transactional, 73; transformational, 94

meditation, ix–xii, xiiin1, xix, xxii, 11, 15, 20, 31, 45, 75, 89, 111, 114, 118, 137–39; benefits of, 143; body scan, 17–18, 48; five senses, 78, 81; log and journal, 86; Metta, 30, 54, 62–65, 118; mindful seeing, 47, 49; transcendental, ix; walking talks, 46; witness, agent, 32, 45, 48–49
mind, ix–xi, xxii–xxiii, 8–9, 11, 15–20, 29, 31, 39, 45, 62–63, 68–69, 71, 75, 78–79, 106–108, 111, 132–35, 137–39, 143, 148; *See also* meditation; unthinkable, 83
multicultural fluency, 70–71, 74
multiplicity, 93, 95

narrative, 37, 47, 52, 56–57, 59, 81, 115; empathy. *See* empathy
National Institute for Civil Discourse, xvi, 147
nervous system, 19, 143; autonomic, xii, 141, 143; parasympathetic, xii; sympathetic, xii

partnership, vii, 73–74
phenotype, 2–3
Post-Black, 5

pranayama, xii, xiiin1, xxii, 137–38;
belly breathing, xii, 19, 64; benefits
of, 142; counting breath, 47;
expanded heart breath, 64; finding
the breath, 19; sharing light, 79, 81;
three-part breathing, 19
privilege, viii, xvii, 1, 10, 25, 27, 34,
108, 110, 121, 123, 126, 129

racial literacy, 10
racism, xvii, xx, xxiii, 1, 6, 10, 12, 32–
35, 42, 91, 122, 125–28; anti-racism,
xvii, 2, 32, 35, 97–98, 148; relations,
91, 102–103, 122; talk, xxi, 9–11,
12n6, 41–42
reciprocity, 73, 94
reflection, xix, xxii, 7, 9, 11, 33, 42, 52,
56–57, 60, 79, 84–85, 88–90, 92–93,
95, 110–11, 147; art-based, 90; Kolb
model, 93

Say Her Name, xvii
self-awareness, xii, 9, 11, 70, 72, 84, 126
service, 70, 79, 81, 94, 114–16, 118–19,
121

social: construction, 56; media, xv, xvii,
xxii, 38–39, 56, 110; science, 6
somatics, xi, xxii, 148
stereotype, xviii, 5, 71, 90, 102, 107–
108, 126–28
stress, x, xix, 11, 65, 72, 92, 137, 143
stories, 51–60, 81, 85, 91, 99, 106, 109,
121–23
storytelling, 15, 54, 56–57, 59
student poster, *99*
syllabus, 24, 29, 32, 56, 85–87, 147

uncomfortable. *See* discomfort

vagus nerve, xii, 19–20
violence, xvii, 8, 132

white educational discourse, 11, 13n9

yoga, ix, xi–xii, xvii–xix, xxii,
10, 131–32, 134, 136–38, 148;
eight-limbs of Ashtanga, 131;
foundational postures, 145, *146*;
Nidra, 18, 20; *Sutras of Patanjali*,
52, 75, 89, 131

About the Author

Tru Leverette, PhD, a certified yoga teacher, works as an associate professor of English and director of Africana Studies at the University of North Florida. Her research interests broadly include race, gender, and identity in literature and culture; yoga practice and philosophy; and mindful pedagogy. Her recent work has been published in *MELUS: Multi-ethnic Literature of the United States*, *Obsidian: Literature in the African Diaspora*, and the edited collections *Other Tongues: Mixed Race Women Speaking Out* and *The Search for Wholeness and Diaspora Literacy in Contemporary African-American Literature*. Dr. Leverette has been a contributing blogger for *Mixed Roots Stories* and is the editor of the collection *With Fists Raised: Radical Art, Contemporary Activism, and the Iconoclasm of the Black Arts Movement*.

www.ingramcontent.com/pod-product-compliance
Lightning Source LLC
Chambersburg PA
CBHW020123010526
44115CB00008B/945